Tompkins County

and

Tammany Hall

"*I have researched the area and talked to highway officials in Lansing and they report there are no large through haul trucks utilizing Lansingville Road. What is using the road is as I thought, Agriculture Vehicles.*"

— *Tompkins County Highway Director*

Tompkins County

and

Tammany Hall

[I can't seem to find any difference at all]

A Circumstantial Case

by

Doug Baird

ISBN 13: 978-1-7359817-2-7 (Paperback edition)

Preface

"Early Sunday morning, June 4, 2017, I was sicker than I had ever been before.

Too sick to even bend over, as I vomited all over the toilet, myself, and the bathroom floor— and I didn't even care.

The previous afternoon, when I was outside mowing the lawn, a high-clearance agricultural boom sprayer sped towards me from an adjoining field and sprayed me with a cloud of a toxic herbicide."

This issue is unresolved; and so are all the other issues and incidents presented in this book. The complete lack of any meaningful or substantive action on the part of authorities in Tompkins County and New York State was a driving force behind writing this book; and my continued efforts to get a positive resolution for the county's marginalized rural community.

My "closure" in writing these narratives was not in the closing of past issues; but in acting to keep those issues open and exposed to public view — and, hopefully, public pressure.

The circumstantial nature of these accusations is greatly strengthened by the singular lack of any contradictory evidence. Every incident recounted has the same "M.O." and points in the same direction. The sole basis for selection was the amount of documentation available through public records and my personal involvement.

Any effective circumstantial case depends on the number of facts that support a single conclusion: I have sometimes sacrificed readability in an effort to present those facts. This is not a fictional story, it's not a "who-done-it" — it's a "what-are-you-going-to-do-about-it?"

There is an old joke about two middle-aged women at a Catskill Resort buffet:

The first woman says, "This food is pretty bad." The second woman replies, "Yes, but there's so much of it."

It's my hope that the amount of useful documentation in this book will ameliorate the quality of the writing.

Doug Baird

Lansingville, *March 20, 2022*

Contents

Introduction

I have tried to keep this book a factual, documented indictment of government misconduct; and I failed. There is no way that I can hide the layers of disappointment and anger at years of failure to bring even a small measure of Social Justice to the rural communities of Tompkins County.

If there are inconsistencies in style and editing; they are intentional — because I did not want to read too closely; and remember too vividly.

The need for Justice is like a glowing coal; still waiting for the fuel to blaze up.

DEADLY DRIFT

If there's a law; and nobody enforces it: Does it actually exist?

Contrary to the blasting media disclosures and quick condemnation that accompany any health debilitating activity in urban precincts; the health and well-being of rural residents is of no importance to authorities or the media, or to those who perpetrate the injury.

As you read this narrative; think about how differently these acts of misconduct would be treated if they occurred in a metropolitan or suburban location.

This incident marked a turning point in my life. After many years of pursuing Rural Social Justice through public hearings, letters, speeches and chasing bureaucratic shadows within the law; I had cause to call on the regulatory and clear-cut legislative intent of County, State, and Federal authorities. This chapter recounts how these people "in a position of public trust" answered that call.

The narrative has been organized into a timeline for clarity; and the names have been withheld to keep the focus on their positions and public responsibilities. Everything is fully documented — it's their actions that tell the story.

06/03/2017 – Day of the Herbicide Poisoning – mid-afternoon – my weather station was reading winds of 16-20 MPH

I was outside on my rider mower, when a high-clearance agricultural boom sprayer entered an adjoining field to the north and sped towards me; spraying me with a cloud of a chemicals.

[These agricultural boom sprayers are designed to ride through fields, above weeds and crops. A typical specification for one of these machines would be: 12 ft. high x 28 ft. long x 12 ft. wide without boom, and 90-120 ft. wide with boom extended. Weight 35,000 lbs. Road speed with boom folded 30-40 mph. Spray application speed with boom unfolded up to 25 mph. A large piece of equipment to use in an area only 300 feet wide.]

At the age of 66; my back stiffens up while seated on the mower and I was unable to get off and move quickly.

I could smell the chemicals as I breathed them in through my mouth and nose.

I immediately went inside and cleaned up and then called the dairy farmer who was renting that field from me to complain – he told me that Helena Chemical was spraying Roundup on that field.

A short time later I received a call from someone at Helena Chemical who informed me that they had spoken with the applicator, but they were rushing to spray before the rain came, and I should take off my clothes and shower — there was not even an apology.

Already cleaned up; with a beer and something to eat; I thought I had put the whole incident behind me.

06/04/2017 – Early Sunday morning

I became aware that I was standing in the middle of the bathroom vomiting all over myself, the toilet and the bathroom floor – and I didn't even care – I remember getting down on my knees and pushing towels around the floor for a while to clean it up, and feeling completely disconnected from what I was doing – then I went back to bed for 24 hours. More than my stomach was outraged – I did not have a bowel-movement for a week afterwards.

I didn't realize at the time how much my physical well-being affected my mental outlook: but after a week or so; my thoughts turned from my interior condition to the conditions of my herbicide poisoning.

06/17/2017 – Complaint

As I felt better; I grew angrier at being sprayed, and more worried about any long term effects.

In spite of advice from neighbors; I submitted a herbicide poisoning complaint to the NYSDEC through their website.

Recounting the incident online brought a number of emotions to the surface; but I tried to keep it a fair and accurate description of the events — it later became evident that I was the only one with that concern.

06/17/2017 – Herbicide poisoning investigated by NYSDEC

Two NYSDEC personnel showed up unannounced: one of them interviewed me while the other took photos outside. I was informed some weeks later that the investigation had been concluded and the case had been disposed; but that if I wanted to see the report; I would need to make a FOIL [Freedom of Information Law] request.

08/15/2017 – The records of the NYSDEC Herbicide Poisoning complaint and investigation are disclosed:

It was my fault.

Government oversight agendas make use of a standard set of fallback protocols to short-circuit complaints and maintain business as usual: Discredit the Person, Discredit the Facts, Discredit the Situation, and It's Legal Anyway. See if you can spot them in this NYSDEC investigative report [names have been withheld, "***" represents redacted text]:

Complaint Form

Facts and Information provided by Complainant

The following information was received through the DEC website "Report an Environmental Violation Online" or sent directly by the complainant to an OPP dispatch mailbox:

Who Did It: Helena

What Occurred: 1 was mowing my lawn, when 1 noticed a large high-clearance ag sprayer racing down the adjacent field towards me. It passed me only a few feet [less than 30 ft.] away and covered me with a strong smelling cloud [I was down wind in a 20 mph wind according to my weather station.] I immediately went inside and tried to clean up, but there was nothing I could do about what 1 had already breathed in and absorbed through my nasal passages, and then called the farmer, J-- C--, who was renting the land. Through the windows I could see the boom sprayer flying around the fields which surround my house on three sides. [There are dead patches in my lawn where overspray has killed the grass.] J-- told me it was herbicide/"round-up', and a short while later someone from Helena called and told me they had spoken with the applicator, but they were rushing to spray before the rain came, and I should take off my clothes and shower — there was not even an apology.

Early Sunday morning, the diarrhea started, followed by fairly severe vomiting a couple of hours later. It took over a week before my digestion seemed back to normal, but the anger still remains.

When Did It Occur: On Saturday, June 3, 2017 in the afternoon [around 3:00 pm]

County: Tompkins Municipality: Lansing

Location Or Address: ___ Lansingville Road

How Did It Occur: Reckless endangerment through arrogance and unsafe application of poison by licensed company.

Additional Details: I'm sure they'll do it again — they're protected by Ag Law.

Date of Submittal: 06/17/2007

On Saturday, June 17th, at approximately 1500hrs, ECO E-- and 1 met with *** at *** residence. A statement was received from

*** indicating that *** leases *** land. approximately 10.5 acres, to J-- C-- for agricultural work. *** stated that on June 3rd, specialized spraying farm equipment sprayed pesticides in a reckless manner by traveling at a high rate of speed, spraying in high winds (20mph from the North read from *** weather station), and by spraying past the cornfield, into *** |adjacent lawn. *** stated that *** was sprayed with the pesticide. and has been violently sick for the following week. *** contacted J-- C-- who said that the chemical was an herbicide, and *** was later contacted by Helena advising *** to remove *** contaminated clothes and shower if *** was sprayed. Overspray of herbicide was found on the south and east edge of the property.

Upon questioning, *** did not seek medical attention for the spraying and I advised *** to do so. *** did not provide an answer for why *** did not report the incident immediately. *** expressed *** views on farming and that | *** was politically active against farming.

06/25/2017 08:05:31

On Wednesday, June 21st, 2017, I visited the C-- Farm located on L-- H-- Rd, T/Lansing. J-- C-- was on vacation, but a farm worker provided the details and contact information for A-- M-- at Helena Chemical. The farm also provided a basic map of pesticide application areas, but was not able to provide a lease for the ___ Lansingville Rd property. 1 contacted A-- and he agreed to meet on Thursday.

On Wednesday. I visited *** as *** was able to find a copy of the lease of the the property Upon investigation of the lease, the lease provided no boundaries or physical descriptors, additionally *** stated that the lease covered 8.5 acres, but *** was leasing the remaining 2 acres on a verbal agreement with J-- C--. The residence and leased farm land are all on one tax parcel. On this visit, I noticed other areas of *** Lawn had dead grass. And **** stated that *** had used roundup herbicide on his lawn.

07/15/2017 14:09:13

On Thursday, the 22nd, I met with A-- M-- of Helena Chemical, applicator # C___. A-- had all required, paperwork and licenses. No previous violations with Helena Chemical. A-- was aware of the complaint and disputed the wind speed and high speed of the tractor and stated that the tractors must travel at 12 mph as the dosage rate is fixed.

Helena Chemical was issued Warning No. 20910 for application of pesticide to non-target area, 6NYCRR 325.2(a)

The complainant was contacted via telephone and notified of the outcome of the investigation.

Case closed!

From negative statements intended to discredit my testimony: "*** did not seek medical attention" - "did not provide an answer for why" – "did not report the incident immediately"; to the ludicrous and false claim that I stated I had used roundup herbicide on my lawn, the whole report seems designed to give the impression that I am evasive, if not an outright liar, acting out of malice and hate. It's a very interesting and revealing response from an NYSDEC investigation that did not even ascertain the wind speed at the time of a herbicide drift complaint.

After dismissing my poisoning; the report spends time quibbling about boundaries and leases. The boundaries were clearly demarked, and unchanged for 20 years

Killing a 3 or 4 foot wide swath of lawn against the strong north winds that were gusting that afternoon would require a boom spraying placement well inside the visible boundaries — a placement that is not consistent with the careful application of herbicide at a speed of "12 mph."

At no point did the NYSDEC's investigation document the actual weather conditions — instead, they merely noted that the applicator "disputed the wind speed". The local NOAA weather station recorded winds of 13-16 MPH with wind gusts of 17 to 23 MPH during that time period – consistent with my own weather station readings. And as I found out later; these boom sprayers are equipped with wind gauges in order to monitor wind conditions while spraying; making it even more suspicious that no actual numbers ever appeared in the report.

The investigators never asked the applicator how, with an unobstructed view from an elevated, glass paneled operator's cabin, he missed seeing me on a rider mower, and continued spraying; driving past me upwind at a distance of less than 50 feet.

And maybe the most egregious aspect; the NYSDEC investigation never made any mention of the restrictions and conditions of this chemical's application under Federal law, or under their own regulatory oversight. The exact chemical brand name was never revealed; but the EPA registration document for "Glyphosate 41%" states:

DIRECTIONS FOR USE

It is a violation of Federal law to use this product in a manner inconsistent with its labeling.

"Do not apply this product in a way that will contact workers or other persons, either directly or through drift. Only protected handlers may be in the area during application."

"Wind – Drift potential is lowest between wind speeds of 2-10 mph."

"Sensitive Areas – The pesticide must only be applied when the potential for drift to adjacent sensitive areas (e.g. residential areas, bodies of water, known habitat for threatened or endangered species, non-target crops) is minimal (e.g. when wind is blowing away from the sensitive areas)."

Further research uncovered additional cautions from leading Agricultural colleges:

University of Minnesota Extension - When is it too Windy to Spray?

- "Always measure wind speed and direction before, during, and after the application. Always follow label information, but in general, wind speeds of 3 to 7 mph are preferable. Spray at low wind velocities (less than 10 mph)."

Perdue University Extension - Reducing Spray Drift from Glyphosate and Growth Regulator

- "Spray when the wind speeds are less than 10 MPH."

- "Spray when the wind direction is away from sensitive areas"

Montana State University Extension - Avoiding Pesticide Drift

- "Spray when the wind speed is 10 mph wind or less."

Michigan State University Extension

- "Professional pesticide applicators carry windspeed gauges to determine if windspeed are within acceptable limits There is no magic number for windspeed though ten miles per hour is a common rule of thumb as a limit for spraying."

• "One the most important cautions on contact herbicide labels is avoid drift."

University of Arkansas Division of Agriculture Research & Extension – Mitigating Pesticide Spray Drift

• "Most labels recommend not applying pesticides when wind is gusty or speed is greater than 10 mph. It is recommended for applicators to regularly and accurately measure wind speed to ensure proper spray deposition."

What was Helena Chemical's motivation? It's the date of the incident that provides an answer. Roundup is sprayed to kill all the vegetation in a field before the corn is planted; and June 3rd is very late for Central New York. That spring was extremely wet, not just in the amount of rain, but in the frequency of showers. In "rushing to spray before the rain" and fulfil contracts within the short window of dry weather; Helena Chemical deliberately ignored government safety and application regulations.

The NYSDEC did not follow even the basic guidelines for an investigation, and never explored the reasons for the event or tried to identify the immediate and underlying causes.

After this door slamming result to my complaint; I posted the NYSDEC report in a detailed blog about my poisoning,

09/02/2017 – Deadly Drift – Emails were sent to the Tompkins County Legislators and the Lansing Town Board; requesting they review the material in the blog.

There was only one response; then no further communication. No action was ever taken.

While I investigated other Rural Social Justice issues; the need to make another attempt at resolving my own herbicide drift issue grew.

I requested local weather records from NOAA for the day of the incident, and took photos of the incident location from the adjoining field that demonstrated an unobstructed view of that location — even at ground level.

I researched label instructions and application regulations and guidelines from authoritative sources [some of which have already been noted.]

In recounting my poisoning incident to others, I found that incidents of herbicide drift and its effects were not uncommon in the community. While one resident mentioned seeing herbicide drifting onto clothes hung out to dry, another was unaware that herbicide had been sprayed and made no connection to the nausea and other symptoms that he experienced until later. Some spoke of the high rate of cancer in their family, and some agreed to come forward and testify.

The NYSDEC report was reviewed by G-- V--, a laboratory and field scientist with twelve years of inspection experience with the NYS DOH and The Cortland County Health department, where he held the title of Environmental Laboratory Consultant and Sanitarian, respectively. He noted the following:

"The first being an investigative report should be FACTUAL, not INTERPETIVE, as in "Expressed views that was politically active against farming." The second was the use of an exclamation point at the end of "case closed" which to me is highly unprofessional, and may be presenting a bias."

My plan was to send an unignorable and fully documented account of the incident to authorities: persuading them to take action.

04/18/2019 – An Express Mail envelope containing the NYDEC Investigation Report, NOAA Climatological Data for the day, an Incident location photo, and a detailed letter describing the case and requesting their help was sent to County, State, and Federal representatives and oversight authorities by Certified Mail.

All of them either did not respond, responded flatly that they "had no authority" or it "did not fall under their jurisdiction" — or referred everything to the NYSDEC for a self-investigation of its own misconduct.

A letter from the Regional Director of the NYSDEC with results of that investigation was forwarded to me, with a cover letter, from my State Representative.

07/08/2019 – "Enclosed find a copy of the correspondence recently received from M-- M--, Regional Director the NYS Department of Environmental Conservation . . . Although the Department's response was not what you hoped for . . ."

The NYSDEC response ignored all the evidence while presenting unsubstantiated arguments for their position:

"DEC has reviewed this matter. For the reasons set forth below, DEC believes that the initial investigation in June 2017 was thorough and the decision not to pursue administrative or criminal enforcement against Helena was proper."

"While it appears that the complainant would like stronger laws, the complaint about DEC'S investigation can only be answered from the perspective of the then current laws and regulations."

The Regional Director even added the text of the regulation that "provides the requirements for use and application of pesticides" — but never explained why the then current regulations were inadequate, or provided any actual figures for the wind speed, pesticide drift, wind direction or proximity to human habitation needed to pursue regulatory enforcement.

The applicator's compliance with Federal label instructions, and the contents of those instructions, was never mentioned. The points brought up by the DOH expert, and all other questions concerning the quality and intent of the original NYSDEC investigation, were never answered or even acknowledged.

The entire response did not include one fact that could be used to hold the Regional Director or the NYSDEC to account for their decisions.

08/01/2019 – A letter sent to my State Representative regarding the inadequacy of the NYSDEC response was not acknowledged.

11/18/2019 – An email follow up complaint to the EPA detailing the case and offering additional information was not acknowledged.

Another spring – I heard loud back-up "beeps" and looked out the window. A high wheel herbicide boom sprayer was carefully backing up, and then moving forward, in the small section of field next to where I was sprayed. This process was repeated for several minutes. It was the first time I had ever seen this behavior, or heard a back-up warning — then I looked across the street and saw someone photographing this display.

If only they had the same level of concern for the health and safety of rural residents.

NON-DISCLOSURE AGREEMENT?

Who are they really helping?

While New York State will only disclose that living in an Agricultural District may expose residents to "activities that cause noise, dust and odors," the United States Court of Appeals for the Second Circuit has expressed the opinion that laws in an Agricultural District "may be inadequate for ensuring the safety of our environment and for protecting citizens from serious injury."

The current *New York Agricultural District Disclosure Form and Notice* helps rural real estate agents sell properties, protects the image of Industrial Farming, and ensures higher assessments for taxing authorities, but its blatant non-disclosure of modern farming methods and iniquitous Agricultural Laws encourage prospective buyers to assume the risks of "serious injury" and financial disaster for themselves and their families — without being made aware that these risks even exist.

New York State refuses to take reasonable steps to ensure that prospective rural property buyers understand the financial and health risks of living in an Agricultural District; so that they are in a position to make an informed decision.

Updating New York's Agricultural District Disclosure Form and Notice is an essential step in obtaining Social Justice for the rural community.

05/20/2019 – a detailed letter pleading the case for the health and well-being of the rural community and requesting help in disclosing the risks of living in an Agricultural District was sent to County and State representatives and oversight authorities by Certified Mail.

All of them either did not respond, responded flatly that they "had no authority" or passed it off to another department where it was never heard of again.

The following text is from the letter:

"I am writing you to request that you update the New York State Agricultural District Disclosure Form and Notice to ensure that prospective buyers understand the financial and health risks of living in an Agricultural District so that they are in a position to make an informed decision.

From the NYS Agricultural District Disclosure Form and Notice:

'This disclosure notice is to inform prospective residents that the property they are about to acquire lies partially or wholly within an agricultural district and that farming activities occur within the district. Such farming activities may include, but not limited to, activities that cause noise, dust and odors.'

The United States Court of Appeals for the Second Circuit [*Mather v. Willet Dairy*] in finding against plaintiffs suffering from the effects of manure off-gassing that included brain damage in one child and the surgical removal of eyelids in an adult commented:

'We recognize that limiting citizen suits in this respect can cause serious injury to persons living near environmental dangers if the DEC and other environmental regulatory agencies are unable to monitor and sanction polluters effectively before compliance deadlines. Given that Willet Dairy had more than seven years before it was required to comply fully with its permit, that means no citizen could have brought a suit over that entire time for CWA violations. Such regulatory agencies may be unable to ensure that polluters are acting in accordance with their compliance schedules, given the numerous violations likely to occur. Consequently, limiting the ability of 'private attorneys general' to bring suit until after compliance deadlines may be inadequate for ensuring the safety of our environment and for protecting citizens from serious injury. But that is the remedy that Congress has provided and to which we are bound.'

Manure lagoons have been shown to harbor and emit over 400 VOCs and toxic gases [including Hydrogen Sulfide and Methane], more than 150 dangerous pathogens [including E. coli, Cryptosporidium and Anthrax], growth hormones, heavy metals, antimicrobials and antibiotics.

Particulate matter from agricultural sources contains up to 100 times the amount of bacteria and fungi as normal air.

CDC Centers for Disease Control and Prevention cites the threat of antibiotic resistance:

'When animals are given antibiotics for growth promotion or increased feed efficiency, bacteria are exposed to low doses of these drugs over a long period of time. This is inappropriate antibiotic use and can lead to the development of resistant bacteria.'

'Resistant germs from the animal gut can also get into the environment, like water and soil, from animal manure.'

Although decades of scientific reports have expressed concern for the health of neighbors impacted by agricultural activities and cited the need for further investigation, no comprehensive or long-term studies have ever been made.

Many Agricultural District wells have been polluted through manure spills and other agricultural activities. Buyers need to be informed that well owners are solely responsible for the safety and quality of their well water [and that remedies, such as reverse osmosis and drinking bottled water are very expensive.]

Prospective buyers need also to be made aware that 'satellite' lagoons containing millions of gallons of liquid manure may be constructed next to rural residences on any land owned or bought by a farm and at the sole discretion of the farmer.

And that in an Agricultural District the 'right of use and enjoyment' of the buyer's property will be effectively subordinated to any agricultural activity designated as a 'sound agricultural practice' by the New York Commissioner of Agriculture and Markets.

From the NYS Agricultural District Disclosure Form and Notice:

'Prospective purchasers are urged to contact the New York State Department of Agriculture and Markets to obtain additional information or clarification regarding their rights and obligations under Article 25-AA of the Agricultural and Markets Law.'

Looking for clarification of risks associated with living in an Agricultural District, I called the number listed on the Ag and Markets webpage. I was answered by an operator at the NYS Dept. of Ag and Markets Call Center. The operator was surprised and said she didn't get calls about this. After a couple of minutes of research, she forwarded me to Land and Water Resources where someone there put me through to another party to answer my questions. He stated it was a 'complicated law' and spoke of 'farmers seeking protection' from towns and neighbors and restrictive laws.

When I pressed him about the health risks, he stated everything was on a 'case by case' basis, and if I identified the parcel there might be some hazardous material sheets, but I should really get in touch with the Agricultural District Coordinator from Cornell Cooperative Extension. Recognizing the name of the Coordinator, and having had issues with that person's assertion that nobody but farmers deserved to live in North Lansing, I stopped the bureaucratic handoff at this point.

According to real estate professionals; this disclosure notice is not presented to a prospective

28

buyer until the time the contract for the offer is being drawn up.

Given the late timing of its presentation, the lack of meaningful disclosure within the Notice itself, and my inability to 'obtain additional information or clarification regarding their rights and obligations' — the NYS Agricultural District Disclosure Form and Notice is a document whose purpose is to limit the warranty of prospective buyers without their knowledge.

If this is an oversight, it can be fixed. If it's deliberate, it's an unconscionable contract.

Please let me know what steps you plan to take to correct this."

An *unconscionable contract* is one that is so one-sided or so unfair that it shocks the conscience. The two main factors that determine unconscionability are both present:

Bargaining power, i.e., oppression - One party will have bargaining power over another party if the disadvantaged party is less knowledgeable in the industry: The increased scope of modern agricultural methods and their serious documented impact on property owners in an Agricultural District is never mentioned.

Unfair terms, i.e., surprise - Another example of unfair terms would be hidden language found in the contract. Such hidden language will almost always constitute unfairness, particularly if the disadvantaged party was unaware of the verbiage in the agreement: The overriding policy of Agricultural Law; that it can subordinate the "right of use and enjoyment" of your property, remove the right of remediation of damage, and the protection of your family from any action deemed a "sound agricultural practice" is never even hinted at in the form's 150 word gloss-over.

08/25/2019 – I emailed the text of the letter [with a copy of the Agricultural Disclosure form attached] to the members of the County Legislature.

After an initial positive response and an indication of willingness to at least add a supplemental County disclosure statement, everything went silent.

11/19/2019 – I received an email stating that the Legislature had handed the matter over to the local Board of Realtors and the County Ag and Farm Protection Committee, both of whom were referred to as the "stakeholders," and that my "concerns and suggestions" had been "passed on." The prospective rural property buyers — in spite of the size of their vested interest, and being the most directly affected; were never referred to as being stakeholders — they were never mentioned at all.

Just as in the Deadly Drift herbicide complaint, the decision to take any action was left in the hands of the same people who had the most to lose if any action on the misconduct was taken. No "conflict of interest" concerns were ever expressed by any County Legislator.

It's the same pattern of behavior that "people in a position of public trust" in New York State exhibit on every rural issue. It's the boot mark of Urban Colonialism.

TRUCK ROUTE

There's an old saying: "Where there's smoke there's fire"; but when you can see flames over the treetops; you don't need a anyone to tell you there's a conflagration – The only question is: Will anybody come to put it out?

The roads in and around the hamlet of Lansingville were quiet rural roads; named after the families that lived on them. What were once backwater roads to nowhere; have become major routes through nowhere; to everywhere – a series of intransigently unregulated short-cuts through a community that doesn't matter to Tompkins County authorities.

In looking over the timeline narrative I've written for this chapter; I realize how tedious reading the repeated negative results may be for the reader — but I wanted readers to understand the frustration, effort, and lack of result that are the hallmarks of citizen-government interaction in Tompkins County. This chapter recounts only part of the efforts, and it's only the first chapter in the story . . .

This is a good a place to start as any:

10/01/2019 – Email to a candidate running for the Lansing Town Board – Dear Ms. B**:

"I received your 'Who do you want for your neighbor' card in the mail and want to reach out to you — to rephrase your campaign slogan: *Your representation can preserve rural Lansing . . . or not.*

In this letter I would like to focus on something that you can do to help preserve the safety and quality of life in Lansing's rural community — have the Lansing Town board request that Tompkins County exclude big trucks from Lansingville Road (CR155)."

The email continued with several pages of documented arguments explaining why these through-cutting trucks are destructive to the roadways and environment, and detrimental to the safety and quality of life of the rural community.

10/08/2019 – Email from County Legislator M** S**:

"A** sent me your email. I read over it, but need to again as there was a lot there. I also forwarded on to our county roads superintendent. His email is below:"

"M**-

Couple of quick thoughts:

Trucks using this road are likely Agriculture or local and there would be no way of limiting either.

If they are Through Haul Trucks I don't understand why they would be using this road? Do you know of any reason?"

10/09/2019 – Email to County Legislator M** S**:

"Thank you for looking into this issue.

Here are a few of my quick thoughts on Mr. S**'s comments:

'Trucks using this road are likely Agriculture or local and there would be no way of limiting either.'

As far as I can see, he has no basis either in fact or through observation of Lansingville Road for making that statement. I work at home in my studio, and I only have to turn my head [and the noise they make is definitely head turning] to have an unobstructed view of Lansingville Road. These are definitely not agricultural trucks. I can see the mounds of gravel in the back, and when traveling down Lansingville they have all three of the back axels down to carry the maximum weight these trucks are capable of.

'If they are Through Haul Trucks I don't understand why they would be using this road? Do you know of any reason?'

Once again, a puzzling reaction from Mr. S**. Why should the reason matter? Maybe it saves five seconds.

Maybe it would annoy people in Genoa if the trucks used Route 90. It could be, as the Cornell report finds, because of safety and weight issues.

Following these trucks through Lansingville Road, and other rural roads, to and from the job sites will quickly substantiate the facts."

10/26/2019 – From County Legislator M** S**:

"J** S** tells me:

"I have researched the area and talked to highway officials in Lansing and they report there are no large through haul trucks utilizing Lansingville Road.

What is using the road is as I thought, Agriculture Vehicles."

11/13/2019 – Email to County Legislator M** S**:

"The attached shows seven different thru haul trucks [clearly none of these trucks are agricultural.] Note that in bottom right hand truck you can actually see the uncovered gravel."

No response or acknowledgement of this email was ever received.

Throughout the winter, spring, and summer; a number of emails were sent to both Town and County authorities: detailing and documenting the deteriorating conditions, and the pressing need for implementing traffic management on the roads around and through Lansingville — these communications were almost never responded to; and never in any meaningful way.

In the fall of 2020; a new attempt was made to bring traffic management to our rural roads and establish a weight limit for non-agricultural through-cutting trucks. We reached out to our County Legislature representative, M** S**, to request that the County Highway Department place a 4-ton weight limit on non-local, through-cutting trucks.

12/03/2020 – From County Legislator M** S** - "This is what I got back from county highway":

"You are correct the State decides on Reduced Speed Zones. The County places weight restrictions and can change centerline road striping.

Large truck wise. This issue has been going on for a while. The weight restrictions will only effect through traffic. Any agricultural or delivery activity will still have the ability to use the road. When we looked into this before on a complaint from Mr. Baird it was found to be Agriculture Trucks cutting the fields. Although they can make a mess of the road with mud, they would not be effected by a road posting

We can look at what exists as far a passing zones, etc and change accordingly next season. That said we are reluctant to change passing zones if we don't see or are aware of some change in the area, ie. New

Homes or businesses that change traffic flow or density in some way.

Please let me know if you have any questions."

12/03/2020 – To County Legislator M** S** and Town Board member A** B**:

"That is a ludicrous assertion from J** S**; as anybody on Lansingville Road can tell you.

Lansingville Road continues to be a thru-cut route for commercial and industrial dump trucks, flatbeds and tractor trailers on a daily basis.

I sent you a montage of some of the dump trucks using Lansingville Road [taken on with an old digital camera], after J** made the last 'agriculture only' statement – and will reattach it."

12/16/2020 – To County Legislator M** S** [to further address the "misidentification" explanation by County Highway Director J** S**]:

"I am well aware of which trucks are 'Agriculture Trucks cutting the fields'; and which are not.

1. They are built different - made for carrying harvest crops, not stones. Gravel, etc. The sides are noticeably higher and different in conformation. [The very few old dump trucks used have plywood added to one side to allow them to be loaded with more by the combine harvester.] Their wheels/tires are made for heavy loads over softer fields.

2. I am familiar with most of the trucks that carry crops on Lansingville Road, and see them parked in the farmyards. Others have "W** Dairy" on the doors.

3. These "Ag Trucks" are only used at intervals to harvest crops; and can be seen and heard on neighboring fields at that time.

4. The most obvious reason: crop trucks are mounded/loaded well above the sides and are not tarped, so it's plain which trucks are carrying crops, and which are not – you can't miss seeing it."

Just before the end of 2020: the Tompkins County Highway Department posted a number of through-truck weight limit signs around Lansingville — for "20 TONS"!

12/31/2020 – To County Legislator M** S**:

"Attached is my brother's photo of the signage on Burdick Hill Road. [Speed limit 40 – Weight limit 4 tons; except local delivery – double yellow line/no passing]

We want nothing that Burdick Hill Road residents [and others] don't already have — and with less reason."

No response or acknowledgement was ever received.

01/06/2021 – To County Legislator M** S**:

"The O'T**, A** C**, and other dump trucks have been roaring up and down Lansingville Road at speed all day - every day this week [untarped], along with flatbeds and other industrial traffic. Crazy, reckless drivers fill the road.

Have you made any progress in getting our traffic concerns addressed?"

No response or acknowledgement was ever received.

01/11/2021 – To County Legislator M** S**:

"Farm tractors towing equipment pass by my window, slowly traveling up and down Lansingville Road; and O'T** and A** C** dump trucks roar by up and down Lansingville Road every weekday at more than twice the speed of these tractors . . . Blatant disregard for any traffic laws by thru-cutters is endemic in our hamlet — everyone now knows there is no law in Lansingville.

Can you please let us know what's being done?"

No response or acknowledgement was ever received.

01/21/2021 – To County Legislator M** S**:

"I was wondering; have you anything in process to help us in managing traffic on Lansingville Road?

It's been over three weeks [since our December 29th meeting] and we haven't heard anything.

My brother has been checking; and every other road with a posted weight limit specifies '4 TONS' and a 2 ton axel weight.

My research shows that '20 TON' weight limit signs are reserved for bridges, not roads."

No response or acknowledgement was ever received.

03/25/2021 – To County Legislator M** S**:

"Nothing has happened with the requested weight restrictions on thru-cutting trucks; the 20 TON sign is still up . . . and my recent emails to the Town and County have not even been acknowledged."

No response or acknowledgement was ever received.

03/30/2021 – Complaint Letter to: L** H**, Deputy County Administrator - Department of County Administration:

"Re: Tompkins County Highway Department

Dear Ms. H**:

I wish to complain in the strongest terms about the response of the Tompkins County Highway Department to our request for a weight limit restriction on non-local trucks.

Commercial and industrial trucks have been using Lansingville Road and the Hamlet of Lansingville as a thru-cut for development projects from BJs to the new Cargill Mine Shaft and the Salmon Creek Bridge work.

These trucks race through, sometimes hundreds of times a day; driving aggressively down the middle of the road, and routinely passing agricultural traffic on the double-yellow lines — creating a serious safety issue.

The repeated heavy-truck traffic is breaking down the narrow [20 wide] paved surface of the road relied upon by local farmers.

They also scour down the dirt and gravel shoulders to as much as several inches below the road surface; creating a dangerous lip for small cars and bicycles.

There is no hardship to the trucking companies; since Lansingville Road is paralleled by state highways on either side.

The County Highway Department Supervisor has the power to set weight limits on local roads; so we asked our County representative, M** S**, to forward our request to have a 4-TON weight limit set on non-local traffic for Lansingville Road.

He received the following response from County Highway Supervisor J** S**:

"I have researched the area and talked to highway officials in Lansing and they report there are no large through haul trucks utilizing Lansingville Road. What is using the road is as I thought, Agriculture Vehicles."

This statement was so at odds with reality that it took us aback. We sent photos of just a few of the many large non-agricultural trucks that are "utilizing Lansingville Road," and sent them to M** S**.

There was no response from the County to our documentation; and at the end of December 2020; signs suddenly appeared on Lansingville Road setting a 20-TON limit on non-local traffic — this is 5 times the weight limit that the County has posted on any other local road. And it's a sign that is usually reserved for bridges, not roads.

Residents are frustrated and angry at the County's dismissive treatment of their request, and the apparent disregard shown for their safety; as well as restricting agricultural activity in a proposed agricultural zone located within a NYS Agricultural District.

How can you fix this?

We want nothing that the residents of many other local roads, like Burdick Hill Road, haven't already have received without demur; and for far less cause."

Enclosures (1): Photo of weight limit sign

04/14/2021 – Reply Letter from: L** H**, Deputy County Administrator - Department of County Administration:

"Dear Mr. Baird:

I received your complaint about the Tompkins County Highway Department and your request for a weight limit restriction on non-local trucks traveling on Lansingville Road.

I spoke with Highway Director J** S** about your concerns. The Highway Director is prohibited from posting roads based solely on citizens' requests;

rather there needs to be data indicating that damage to the road has occurred because of heavier loads.

In regard to Lasingville Road, Mr. S** posted the road at 20 tons to limit through traffic of large trucks. This came in part from your previous request for a weight restriction because the data did indicate that road is in poor shape, and the weight limit would help to prevent it from deteriorating faster. It's important to note that agriculture vehicles and local deliveries are exempt from the posting. This exemption for agricultural vehicles and local deliveries would also be true of a 4 ton weight restriction.

In response to your concerns, and in an effort to better understand the situation, the Highway Department will conduct another traffic count on Lansingville Road in the coming weeks and will utilize this data for related decisions."

04/18/2021 – Email from County Legislator M** S**:

"I know the administration is now looped into the issue on your road. I'm not sure there's a solution. I'll call J** again tomorrow on it."

04/19/2021 – Follow-up letter to L** H**, Deputy County Administrator - Department of County Administration:

Re: Tompkins County Highway Department

"Dear Ms. H**:

Your letter of April 14, 2021 neither responds to, nor accounts for, the actions and assertions of Tompkins County Highway Department Director J** S**; which are the substance of our complaint:

1.   It does not account for his denial of any non-agricultural large truck traffic on Lansingville Road in an email to County Legislator M** S**; in spite of overwhelming evidence to the contrary.

2.   It does not substantiate his claim of research, or give the name of the Lansing Highway Department personnel this assertion is based on.

3.   It does not account for the posting of a 20 TON weight limit without informing County Legislator

M** S**; who was inquiring into this issue as an official County representative.

4.   It does not account for the posted weight limit being five times the [4 TON] weight limit of every other sign posted locally to "limit through traffic of large trucks" — a 20 TON weight limit that would allow the continued high-volume through traffic of gravel trucks — truck traffic that Director J** S** asserts does not even exist.

The County's actions and response do not in any way "maintain public confidence" or meet the needs of local residents. Your letter will be kept on file as documentation for future inquires."

No response or acknowledgement was ever received.

05/06/2021 – Email to Tompkins County legislators:

"I wish to complain in the strongest terms about the response of the Tompkins County Highway Department to our request for a weight limit restriction on non-local, non-agricultural trucks, and the handling of our complaint by Deputy County Administrator L** H**.

[Attached are the ethics complaint to Ms. H**, her response, and my follow up letter.]

All we asked for is what many other local roads already have — how did Burdick Hill Road, Cherry Road and many other local roads get a "4 Ton" weight limit? And why can't we get it the same way?

All we get are obstructions on top of obstructions, deliberate misunderstandings, and answers to requests we never made.

The roads around Lansingville already have considerable large and heavy traffic in the tractors, trucks and agricultural equipment used in today's consolidated farming activities — traffic that none of these other roads have."

"The lack of transparency and inappropriate responses by the Highway Department and the Deputy County Administrator have no place in ethical government.

We look forward, hopefully, to the posting [and enforcement] of 4 ton limits for all non-agricultural thru-cutting trucks on the agricultural roads of our historic hamlet: Lansingville Road, Lockerby Hill Road, and Jerry Smith Road."

No response or acknowledgement was ever received.

05/11/2021 – Email to County Legislator M** S**:

"Do you know if the County Legislators are going to do anything about the thru-cutting trucks . . ?"

No response or acknowledgement was ever received.

05/18/2021 – Email to the Lansing Town Supervisor and the Lansing Town Board, with a request to take action and forward to all Lansing Ag Committee members, and to representative J** K** of NYS Dept. of Agriculture:

"Lansingville Road, Lockerby Hill Road, and Jerry Smith Road have been turned into some of the biggest unregulated high-speed shortcuts and industrial truck routes in Tompkins County [attached is a video of the everyday behavior of thru-cutting traffic on Lansingville, taking place on a curve with a double yellow line; this behavior is also common with dump trucks, tractor trailers, and even Lansing Town trucks.]

The ability to change this is up to you.

Some of us are trying to trying to make our roads a safe and lawful part of the rural community by establishing a 40 MPH speed limit, no passing, a 4-Ton weight limit on non-agricultural, non-local delivery trucks, and enforcement of these laws.

We approached M** S**, our County Representative, and asked him to request that the County Highway Dept. to put a 4-Ton weight limit for non-local deliveries on Lansingville Road. The troubling response by the County is documented in the attached.

County Legislators have, to this day, refused to investigate, explain, or even acknowledge any communication concerning the Highway Department's and Deputy County Administrator's actions, or admit that non-ag trucks use Lansingville Road."

The email continued with additional arguments and points; and ended with a plea for them to get involved – "This is a chance to do good for everyone in the rural community."

Attached were copies of the 3/30/21 complaint letter to the Deputy County Administrator, the 4/14/21 response from Deputy County Administrator, the 4/19/21 follow-up letter to the Deputy County Administrator, the text of the 5/6/21 email to the County Legislature, and a video clip of traffic on Lansingville Road from the previous day.

No response or acknowledgement was ever received from any of the parties.

05/20/2021 – Email to County Legislator M** S** and Town Board member A** B**:

"Could you find out what requirements the residents of Burdick Hill Road, Cherry Road, and the other local roads fulfilled to get approval for their "4 Ton" weight limit postings?

I'm sure we can do the same."

05/25/2021 – Email from Town Board member A** B**:

"Doug...I think this is a positive step to take to reduce large truck traffic.

M** [County Legislator]...Do you know who should be contacted?

A**"

No response or acknowledgement was ever received.

05/29/2021 – Email to Town Board member A** B**:

"I have letters and emails on this issue going back to 2018; and not a single thing has been done to remediate the situation. Are we being stonewalled? If so, why?"

No response or acknowledgement was ever received.

06/01/2021 – Email to County Legislator M** S**:

"Do you have any information yet on what requirements the residents of Burdick Hill Road, Cherry Road, and the other local roads fulfilled to get approval for their "4 Ton" weight limit postings?"

No response or acknowledgement was ever received.

06/07/2021 – Email to County Legislator M** S**:

"Is there anything of substance happening with the request to post a 4-Ton limit on thru-cutting trucks . . ?"

Video clips of dump trucks filled with crushed stone using the road that morning were attached.

No response or acknowledgement was ever received.

06/09/2021 – Email to Town Board member A** B** [owner of a thousand acre dairy farm with permanent easement]:

"I don't know what luck you have had in obtaining any sort of traffic management on our rural roads, but I haven't. More than 4 years of factual and reasoned attempts have gotten me nothing but runarounds, and when I persisted; a stone wall of silence."

"There are three areas in which I see a possible solution, if you are willing to help:

1.   You can act on this issue with the Ag Committee and Town Board – both the Town and County approved the Lansing Ag Protection Plan that lists in its "Goals and Strategies to Preserve

Farmland and Promote Agriculture" a number of recommendations; from "giving priority to farming" to "review traffic/speed limits/signage in agriculture areas to improve safety" and the "maintenance of roads & bridges - for heavy ag vehicles."

2.   J** K** . . . I was told by the Counsel's Office that he is the contact for NYS Ag in this matter.

3.   Help with a petition – once again, you have connections, locally and through the Ag Committee, to get "door to door" and email signatures to a petition. Attached is a sample of what I thought might be wanted."

No response or acknowledgement was ever received.

06/17/2021 – A letter and enclosures were sent to Attorney General Letitia James:

"Re: Tompkins County Government Misconduct

Dear Attorney General James:

I am writing you to request an investigation into the conduct of Tompkins County Highway Director J** S**, as well as the conduct of L** H**, Deputy County Administrator in her handling of an ethics investigation of Director S**'s actions, and the Tompkins County Legislature's subsequent refusal to take appropriate steps to insure ethics and transparency in County government."

The letter contained a detailed account of the actions of the parties named; and enclosed copies of the email response from the County Highway Director, the letter to the Deputy County Administrator, the response from Deputy County Administrator, and a photo of weight limit sign.

The Certified Mail receipt was dated June 21, 2021.

No response or acknowledgement of the letter was ever received.

06/23/2021 – Email to a neighboring town Superintendent of Public Works:

"We want to stop the through-cutting of large trucks. Lansingville Road has become a major route for industrial and commercial traffic from Cayuga County. During projects like the Cargill mine shaft there were hundreds of trucks going back and forth in a day with crushed stone. There are also tractor trailers, heavy equipment flatbeds, and cement mixers that uses Lansingville on a regular basis. There are no law enforcement patrols on Lansingville Road; and these trucks drive aggressively down the middle of the road and routinely pass tractors and farm equipment on the double yellow lines. This narrow road with only gravel shoulders is really taking a pounding as well. There are state highways on either side (34 & 34B) and no hardship or need to use Lansingville Road.

We want to fulfill all the requirements that other residents did and get the same protections."

06/23/2021 – Email reply from the Superintendent of Public Works – Re: Requirements for a "4-ton" weight limit on non-local traffic:

"Residents don't decide where signs are placed. Petitions hold no merit.

Roads are posted for other reasons.

Good luck"

07/05/2021 – Email to County Legislator M** S**:

"I'm still trying every door on a thru-cutting weight limit on Lansingville's roads" . . .

No response or acknowledgement was ever received.

07/07/2021 – Email to All Tompkins County Legislators:

"We are still trying a to get 4-Ton weight limit for thru-cutting trucks on Lansingville's roads; and want to find out how the residents of many other local roads were able to do this. We got this response from one government authority:

'Residents don't decide where signs are placed. Petitions hold no merit.

Roads are posted for other reasons.'

There cannot be a set policy; because there has never been any mention of a policy to date, so it must be decided by a group — who are the people who make this decision?

Even a minimal government transparency should allow citizens to find that out."

Two months later – there was still no response from any Tompkins County Legislator.

Throughout the entire process, and in the face of irrefutable documentary evidence; the County has never changed their claim that these trucks do not even exist.

Once again; the County has given the cold-shoulder runaround to the real needs of the rural community – and they're so comfortable in their power – they don't even try to hide it.

THE PROBLEM

There is a public relations problem that comes pre-packaged with every Tompkins County government agenda: *Why does every policy decision work to the benefit of Cornell University?*

The *"All of Us Together"* concept of "Tompkins County" was created to mold the surrounding towns and villages into a pattern that is beneficial to Cornell's corporate growth — it has no other purpose.

"Tompkins County" government doesn't work with the people – it works with the corporations, the institutions, the politicians, bureaucrats, and special interests.

They are *power brokers.*

That's why the county's public policies are never decided in the public sector — it's not a government of the people – it's a government *above* the people.

"Tompkins County's" decision making flow chart is a beautiful example of Vertical Integration: every stage of government action is integrated and controlled from the top.

It's the very strength of this system that makes it so easy to spot – and once spotted; its methods of public "predation" can be studied:

Camouflage – Cornell moves everywhere among the shadows – policies are carried out by them, because of them, or in gratitude to them. Even when the "County" claims its concerns are with the people – Deferential nods are given to Cornell's "importance".

Media stories read like the handouts that they are; and if public opposition forces the reporting of a community or environmental outcry – the article always ends with rebuttals of those concerns; at length.

Deal making – as exampled by the Town of Lansing's Comprehensive Plan and Agriculture Protection Plan: this once rural town was divided into two distinct land uses to appease the county's powerful Development and Agricultural interests. Not only do both plans dovetail perfectly and express wholehearted support of each other as an important part of their own plan's success — both were written by Cornell.

Credentials – every policy "push" releases a flood of credentials – even if they know nothing about the particular community or the needs of residents: they know exactly how to solve every problem — you do what "Tompkins County" wants. [If you want to have career longevity.]

Beneficence – while I have never met a single resident or employee who believes that altruism plays a part in the University's corporate agenda – their dictator-inspired "parades" and proclamations are a not-to-be-gainsaid part of Cornell's "Sun King" persona.

Meaningless public participation – public participation is kept to a minimum: none. Tompkins County fosters rulership; not representation. At Lansing Town meetings the public cannot ask any questions; and are told they're lucky to even be allowed to speak.

Power – Cornell is more than just a big frog in the small pond of Tompkins County – it's a big frog that swallowed the county. Connected at all levels of government and business, even internationally; they are the controlling authority for *every* activity within the county.

On the workplace level there's "Cornell Paranoia": The fear of being associated with any thought, belief, or person that makes your superiors unhappy – even a social media link or the mention of a critical observation might get back to the hierarchy and result in your losing your job — it's "old school" palace intrigue in a new millennium setting.

Stone walling – If you ask unwelcome questions, or persist in opposition – the County just shuts down; and refuses to communicate or acknowledge your existence. It's a further proof of the power behind County government that they can do this and get away with it.

Enhancing Cornell's power and profit is what Tompkins County government does — *it's what they are.*

The reader may find this essay a bit "offhand" for the seriousness of the subject; but it's intended to be descriptive of the situation, and not a rigorous examination.

It's something to keep in mind when you're presented with a County "bill of goods."

WHOSE PLAN IS THIS ANYWAY?

At first glance; the County's "vision" reads like a Visitor Center brochure — but a more thorough inspection reveals authoritarian boot marks among its carefully worded phrases:

"THE TOMPKINS COUNTY COMPREHENSIVE PLAN presents a vision for the future of the community. It is based on a set of principles that reflect the values of the community as expressed by the County Legislature they have elected. The Plan seeks to foster a place where individual rights are protected while recognizing the benefits that can accrue to community members from common actions. It largely focuses on voluntary collaboration between the public and private sectors, but also supports the role that local regulation can play in addressing key issues impacting the entire community and helping people to live together in harmony. Where regulation is required, it should balance the burdens placed on individuals and businesses with the restrictions needed to protect or otherwise benefit the larger community. In most cases the Plan seeks to expand

individual choice in terms of where and how people live their lives."

Their rosy "vision for the future" displays an underlying elitist policy making attitude:

•   It reflects the "values of the community" but only "as expressed by the County Legislature."

•   It claims to "foster a place where individual's rights are protected" but in the same sentence subordinates this to "common actions."

•   It "focuses on voluntary" but "supports the role of local regulation."

•   And while the County's Plan states: *"Where regulation is required, it should balance the burdens placed on individuals and businesses with the restrictions needed to protect or otherwise benefit the larger community"* it nowhere indicates who will decide what these "regulations" and "burdens" are – and how they will be implemented.

By removing those· portions of their "vision" statement that are negated by qualifiers; we arrive at a more straightforward disclosure of intent:

This plan is based on values that reflect the principles of the County's Legislature. In serving this agenda; We will choose the burdens to place on individuals and businesses, and decide which individuals to restrict in their choice of where and how they can live.

Corroboration of this interpretation is provided by statements like: *"The Plan includes policies that, when considered together, can help create both rural and urban communities"* — exposing the County's intention to *"create"* new communities, rather than help those that already exist.

What these new communities will be like and who will benefit from their creation is a connecting thread in this Comp Plan "deconstruction."

Like many speeches of grandiose rhetoric; the writers can't help but leave a trail of truth in their efforts to cover it up. The County may claim to be "helping people to live together in harmony" – but harmony requires more than one voice, and that's something that is entirely missing from the Tompkins County Comprehensive Plan.

WHOSE PLAN IS THIS ANYWAY?

Part 2

While the Tompkins County Comprehensive Plan claims that it's only a guide; and readily admits that "New York State clearly places land use authority in the hands of its towns, villages, and cities" – the reality of the County's methods undercuts its pretentions of local community control and ethical good faith.

New York Town Law § 272-a – Legislative findings and intent:

"The legislature hereby finds and determines that: Among the most important powers and duties granted by the legislature to a town government is the authority and responsibility to undertake town comprehensive planning" and that town government should *"assure full opportunity for citizen participation in the preparation of such proposed plan"*

But the Tompkins County Comp Plan urges local municipalities renounce that duty and to deny citizens participation in planning:

"Often, local municipalities have a full workload simply addressing the important day-to-day issues of local concern. Planning at the county level can help municipal governments address key issues of concern that cross municipal boundaries"

In the face of the legislative intent set out in New York Town Law: How can the County ethically even make such a suggestion?

More and more; Tompkins County Legislators are taking an aggressive "hands on" approach to making their own "vision" – everyone's reality:

Tompkins County Action Items Adopted: 2019

Action Item #1 *"Undertake direct outreach and engagement with municipalities several times each year to identify opportunities to assist their implementation of projects that would directly promote the policies of the Tompkins County Comprehensive Plan"*

Their own words and actions demonstrate the County's intent to be much more than a "guide" – and are part of an ongoing attempt to coerce local municipalities into renouncing their lawful responsibilities — and to gather all power and control into the centrality of vested interests.

WHOSE PLAN IS THIS ANYWAY?

Part 3

"A lie that is half-truth is the darkest of all lies." –
Alfred Tennyson

The only thing more indigestible than Tompkins County's refusal to allow residents meaningful participation in County government; is the County's pretense of enabling public participation. The Tompkins County Comprehensive Plan's "Listening to Community Voices" is a laughably unconvincing cover story; dismissively penned by those who are unconcerned with whether you believe it or not.

From Kickoff Survey:

"Tompkins County needs YOUR INPUT to help develop the scope of the Comprehensive Plan Update."

"The purpose of this survey is to gather input on what should be covered in the update to the Tompkins County Comprehensive Plan.

However; the "ten elements already included in the Comprehensive Plan" by Tompkins County legislators, before the first community survey was even announced – are unchanged in the final document. The Comp Plan is a "revealed" document, not a participatory one.

The "kickoff survey" was a vague, generalized survey that used loaded terms like "Healthy Communities" to fish for results that would support policies that the County had already decided on. [Who wouldn't vote for a healthy community?]

The two additional topic areas that were "identified" [from a list of thirteen possible choices supplied by the County] made no meaningful difference to the final County Plan.

"APPENDIX B – Public Comments and Responses" [not included in the Tompkins County Comp Plan document] shows how the County reacted to actual "Voices of the Community":

Comments:

"Can there be a policy that prioritizes transportation investments for the 'transportation insecure' –

especially low-income families with children in rural areas."

"I think it's important to pay attention to the needs of rural residents. In addition to fixed-route what is possible as a systematic approach to meeting public transit needs."

The County responded with the following "substantive change":

"Proposed Policy: Consider the needs of populations that are particularly challenged by transportation when developing systems and alternatives."

Note that County policy will only "consider" the needs, rather than "meet" the needs – and they refuse to acknowledge that rural residents have special problems or needs by excluding the mention of "rural" from their policy statement. The tag line of "alternatives" is used to hide the County's real policy agenda – that the rural disabled and elderly are forced to rely on friends and neighbors, try to book a volunteer driver, or pay for expensive taxi service — or somehow travel the miles to their "Ag Ghetto" border; and wait on the side of the road for a TCAT bus.

Tompkins County's rural population pays the same County taxes at the same rate as the rest of the county; but does not receive services like transportation and law enforcement — this is blamed on "the high cost of rural service and constrained fiscal resources" by the County — while at the same time, in a neighboring community only a few miles away; the buses stop every few hundred feet – and at tax exempt Cornell University; with students who only pay the occasional sales tax — there are so many buses in service that I'm told that it's very difficult to drive around the campus.

Comment:

"Overarching principle – looking out for rural landowners (Broaden the idea so people are as important as the rest of it.) All residents matter/ every resident matters."

County response:

"A Foreword was added to explain how the principles, policies and actions of the Comprehensive Plan can contribute to a positive future for both urban and rural residents of the County."

The Plan's Foreword clearly shows that it is the principles, policies and actions of the County's "vision" that are important – not the people. Tompkins County Legislators subordinate human worth to powerful interests and inflexible doctrine in every Comprehensive Plan policy.

Comments:

"The assumption that 'planners' can design and provide the most desirable lifestyle for the most people is pure hubris."

"This document is nothing more or less than an attempt to have the government control everything."

"The questions suggest their own answers, those planners want to hear. They are designed to steer the outcome into a pre-ordained mold, subordinating individual choices to government control."

County response:

"Many residents of the County appreciate the vision presented in this plan but some fear that it can only be achieved by more regulation and what is perceived as increased intrusion by government into their lives.

The Foreword explains how local regulation has a role to play but that the County does not have such direct regulatory authority over most areas addressed in the plan and the plan relies heavily on voluntary actions by individuals and organizations that the County may be able to collaborate with."

There is no evidence to support the statement that "Many residents of the County appreciate the vision presented in this plan" — The overwhelming perception of residents is that Tompkins County government is corrupt and that there is no meaningful public participation: and with a new comprehensive plan "vision" that boldly announces where and how everyone should live — "increased intrusion by government into their lives" is anything but a "perception" for Tompkins County residents.

The plan's thin excuse of policy "guidelines" does little to cloak the ambition that is revealed in the last sentence of their response – Tompkins County government has no intention of allowing any "plan" but their own.

Comment:

"Efforts to acquaint citizens with this plan which will, by design, touch each and every resident of Tompkins County are pitiful to non-existent. There were 4 meetings attended by a total of 70 individuals out of a Tompkins County population of 101,570."

"In a survey to critique the TC Plan conducted in the fall of 2013 there were 915 responses of .9% of the county population. Of these, a large number [more than 25%] were from Participation in Government classes in four local high schools. The session with Planning Department officials I attended earlier this month in the TC Library also seemed poorly attended.

This is a laughable attempt at having an informed electorate. Yet, this plan will be voted on nevertheless."

County response:

"Listening to Community Voices describes the considerable efforts to involve the public at three separate stages in preparing the Comprehensive Plan."

In truth: very little effort was made to involve the public, and their comments and concerns had no impact of any substance on principles and policies already decided upon "in house." The 915 survey responders did nothing more than choose which of the preselected "topic areas" were preferred [while the Planning Advisory Board made the actual choice] — it was participation on the level of "Do you want to have mac and cheese on Tuesday? Or Wednesday?"

And in what the County describes as "Another major public outreach effort" in the spring of 2014 – a total of "over 70 individuals" attended six meetings. [A pathetic number for any public meeting.]

The County's Comprehensive Plan states that "the Department sent information and requests for input to a wide variety of email addresses" – but only mentions "local government officials, advisory board members, and previous commenters" — and by posting "information about the public meetings" to the "Department's Facebook and Twitter accounts" – they would again reach the same limited group already involved.

Comments and questions were solicited at meetings of County advisory boards, Business and economic development groups, Local government groups, and undisclosed "Groups the Department has worked with over the years" — once more gathering input from the county's power structure.

In spite of the obviously inadequate response from the public; no effort was made in the local media or community outreach to rectify this situation, or to solicit public approval of the Plan's policy statements.

The legitimacy of Tompkins County's "LISTENING TO COMMUNITY VOICES" pastiche of public participation is based solely on their own assertions that it is so.

Few of the county's residents were even aware that a new comprehensive plan was being prepared — and that was according to plan as well.

WHOSE PLAN IS THIS ANYWAY?

Part 4

Rural Colonization

Definition of *Urban Colonialism*

1 : of, relating to, characteristic of, or constituting control by a city over a rural area or people

2 : a policy advocating or based on such control

In trying to write about the Tompkins County Comprehensive Plan [as with many other recent plans] I am confronted with the difficulty of untangling the mass of misrepresentations and lies that provide the underpinning for their policy agenda.

Just one Policy sentence may misrepresent the cause, current situation, the impact, the population, the intent, and the viability of the solution that the Plan proposes — making it almost impossible to get to the bottom of an issue; or even follow a single thread.

As a starting point for this essay; I searched for the word "rural" – and found it appeared 84 times in the County's Comprehensive Plan.

Grouping sentences where it appears; a pattern emerges:

"In rural areas the Plan envisions a working landscape of farms and forests providing products and jobs that support a strong rural economy - Rural economic activities may include businesses processing agricultural and forest products, and other small businesses appropriate to a rural setting - Employment choices for those interested in living and working in rural areas will include full- and part time farming, independent "homestead" lifestyles, entrepreneurship in agricultural and forest product processing, and at-home workers who want to live close to nature – Rural areas will gain economically from urban markets for food, wood products, and energy - Urban areas will have access to the natural beauty, outdoor recreation, and local food and energy provided by our rural landscape - working rural landscapes are preserved"

If this echoes the colonial policies of the 1700's that enforced North America's role as a provider of agricultural goods and raw materials [and a captive consumer of manufactured articles]; it's no coincidence:

Ithaca is not a business center – it is THE Business Center for Tompkins County:

"The Downtown Ithaca Alliance works to maintain and develop downtown Ithaca as the county's center for 'banking and finance, business and professional offices, government and community services, downtown residences, and as a retail destination.'"

"The urban area will include the lively, active downtown and vibrant waterfront district of Ithaca, neighborhood centers serving nearby residents, and regional commercial centers that serve the needs of both urban and rural populations."

"The urban center is the historic employment, retail, service, and government center for the surrounding region"

When the Town of Lansing requested NYSEG to supply a natural gas line needed to attract businesses – Tompkins County Legislators went to the State Capitol and lobbied to block any new natural gas use on environmental grounds. They succeeded.

Shortly thereafter; Cornell proposed building a 1,200 student living complex, powered by natural gas – it was approved without any demur by both the County Legislature and planning authorities.

Then what *is* the land use that County's planners "envision" for rural towns like Lansing?

Colonial resettlement, of course:

"DEVELOPMENT FOCUS AREAS STRATEGY - This strategy identifies an urban center, five established nodes, two emerging nodes, and eight rural centers as the Development Focus Areas

COUNTY ROLE. It is envisioned in the future at least two-thirds of all new residential development would occur in the Development Focus Areas. Tompkins County's role is three-fold in achieving this vision: providing support to municipalities as they undertake these activities; strongly advocating for appropriate types of development within Development Focus Areas and rural land uses outside of the focus areas; and addressing the intermunicipal aspects of implementation, such as providing public transit services to the focus areas, focusing infrastructure investment in the focus areas, and promoting efforts to provide strong pedestrian and bicycle connections between the focus areas and nearby existing developed areas."

By "strongly advocating" the creation of satellite "mini-cities" for their urban workforce, surrounded by rich corporate Agribusinesses [employing tax-subsidized foreign "guest" workers] the County has radically altered the rural landscape – and left no place for the county's rural residents:

"Tompkins County contains an uncommon mixture of spectacular natural features, a vibrant urban center, internationally renowned academic institutions, and a productive and attractive working landscape."

With nearly 60 percent of rural residents calling unemployment a "critical" problem in a community needs assessment survey conducted by the United Way and Human Services Coalition of Tomkins County — The County's planners propose no solution; nor see any need for one.

In the Tompkins County Comprehensive Plan's "vision for the future" – the already marginalized native rural community *will no longer even exist.*

WHOSE PLAN IS THIS ANYWAY?

Part 5

ENVIRONMENTAL ETHICS

It's ethics that gives a government legitimacy

There's a big piece missing from the planning agenda in Tompkins County: *What needs to be done about the environmental destruction caused by modern farming methods?* — and in a not-so-surprising coincidence: this same issue is missing from the County's Comp Plan as well.

The "Environment" section of the Comprehensive Plan holds up Agriculture as a model of stewardship and conservation; while suppressing any mention of the agricultural methods and regulatory exemptions that have made them the biggest polluters in Tompkins County — tiptoeing around their role in the impairment of our water resources and depletion of the ecosystem in a blatant example of cronyism and skewed environmental reporting.

The presentation of some of the arguments is a bit technical; the facts are unequivocal.

The County Comp Plan:

"Fall Creek, Cayuga Inlet, and Sixmile Creek play a significant role in determining the quality of water in the southern basin of Cayuga Lake as they contribute approximately 40 percent of all the surface water entering the southern end of the lake."

Comments:

Salmon Creek also enters the southern part of Cayuga Lake in Tompkins County and drains one of the three largest watersheds in the Cayuga basin.

"The watershed land uses range from the highly urban and forested Cayuga Inlet to the mostly agricultural Salmon Creek."

Nutrient pollution from runoff and groundwater discharge "are relatively minor in the urbanized watershed but are much more significant in the two more agricultural watersheds, Fall Creek and Salmon Creek. The high contributions from groundwater in those watersheds, 55% and 72%, respectively, pose difficult challenges for management because only long-term changes in land use can reduce these loads." — *Nutrient Loads to Cayuga Lake, New York: Watershed Modeling on a Budget, 2012*

Salmon Creek is never mentioned in any of the Comprehensive Plan's water quality discussions; and *agricultural nutrient pollution* is never mentioned at all.

The County Comp Plan:

"Most of the phosphorus that enters the southern end of Cayuga Lake is bound up with the sediment carried by Fall Creek, Cayuga Inlet, and Sixmile Creek. This sediment is largely the result of stormwater runoff and erosion of stream banks."

Comments:

Actually, the percentage of bioavailable particulate phosphorus [available nutrient for algae growth] measured in Salmon Creek was more than twice that of Fall Creek, and more than three times that of both Cayuga Inlet, and Six Mile Creek. [*Phosphorus Bioavailabiltiy and Loads, Upstate Freshwater Institute, 10/22/2015*]

The County Comp Plan:

"Impaired water bodies and their related pollutants, are published by the New York State Department of Environmental Conservation (NYSDEC). The most recent list published in 2012 identified the southern end of Cayuga Lake as impaired by three pollutants: phosphorus, silt/sediment, and pathogens."

Comments:

Phosphorus

"Mean annual TP [Total Phosphorus] load to Cayuga Lake is just under 100 Mg/year, of which 60 Mg/year is DP [Dissolved Phosphorus.] The largest source of both DP and TP is agricultural runoff, providing 45% of the DP and 47% of the TP. Urban runoff provides 13% of the TP but negligible DP. The largest urban TP source, at 8%, is high-density impervious residential land." — *Nutrient Loads to Cayuga Lake, New York: Watershed Modeling on a Budget, 2012*

Silt/sediment

The County's Plan makes no mention of the widespread agricultural practice of "tiling" fields [installing subsurface drainage on the entire field]. Tiling will drain a field in minutes, rather than hours; not only causing water to flow into streams more quickly and allowing less water to replenish the groundwater, but increasing the flow of sediment and manure into Cayuga Lake's tributaries.

Pathogens

The County's Comp Plan makes no mention of agriculture as a source of pathogens.

"My results allow me to conclude that the most nutrient and pathogen pollution occurs after large rainstorm events, especially after manure has been applied to land for months with no precipitation events, and after manure application on frozen ground. These results support the findings from similar studies. I can also generalize that many of the soils from the field sites that I collected from had buildups of phosphorus, which likely contributed to the high concentrations of phosphorus in the runoff samples that I collected. I can also conclude that the manure pathogens that I examined for antibiotic resistance were resistant to high levels of ampicillin. This result further supports the severity of antibiotic resistance and the negative health effects and environmental effects that they can cause." — *"The Effects that Liquid and Solid Cattle Manure have on the Water Quality of Drainage Ditches in Putnam County, Ohio"*, Bowling Green State University, Janelle Horstman, 2014

"Increased phosphorus levels were also detected after precipitation in the agriculturally impacted areas, and fecal coliform densities were much higher after precipitation. The strong correlation of turbidity, total phosphorus, and fecal coliform densities suggests a common source for these parameters. Elevated total phosphorus, turbidity, and fecal coliform densities are presumed to be the direct result of runoff from nearby tiled fields sprayed with liquid manure as reported by MDNRE in numerous previous waste discharge infractions by the CAFO farms in close proximity to our AI sites (Michigan Department of Environmental Quality 2003a, 2004b)." — *"Antibiotic Resistance, Gene Transfer, and Water Quality Patterns Observed in Waterways near CAFO Farms and Wastewater*

Treatment Facilities" West; Liggit; Clemans & Francoeur, 2009

The "Point Source" Smokescreen

The County Comp Plan:

"New York State regulates pollution discharge into waters through its State Pollutant Discharge Elimination System (SPDES) permit program, including the control of all point source discharges to surface waters. The program is designed to maintain water quality consistent with public health, public enjoyment of water bodies, protection and propagation of fish and wildlife, and industrial development in the state."

Comments:

The County fails to mention that this program does not adequately regulate pollution from agricultural sources:

"The Clean Water Act provides a comprehensive regulatory scheme for many discharges of pollutants to waters of the United States. Through the primarily regulatory NPDES permitting program, significant improvements have been made to the quality of the country's water bodies. However, the NPDES permitting program only applies to point sources discharges, thus most agricultural discharges are not subject to permitting or other federal regulatory control. Nonpoint sources, including those from agriculture, remain the most significant water quality challenge facing the nation. Moreover, the CWA's exemption from section 404 permitting for normal farming practices continues to allow many wetlands to be degraded by agricultural activities. Because the CWA does not provide direct federal authority for regulating many agricultural sources of water pollution and wetlands degradation, the responsibility for addressing water quality degradation from agricultural activities has fallen largely to the states. To date, most programs designed to address agricultural water pollution have been voluntary or incentive-based programs designed to encourage farmers to implement best management practices. These programs have been only minimally successful, and agricultural pollution continues to be one of the most significant sources of water quality degradation in the United States, meaning that there is a need for a more comprehensive regulatory system to address the water impacts of farming." — *"Maintaining a Healthy Water Supply While Growing a Healthy Food Supply: Legal Tools for Cleaning Up Agricultural Water Pollution"* Mary Jane Angelo, Professor of Law & Director, Environmental and Land Use Law Program University of Florida Levin College of Law

Stormwater Runoff and Flooding

The County Comp Plan:

"Increased stormwater runoff has a significant impact on floodplain management. As land area is converted to more urbanized uses, the amount of impervious surface associated with that land use generally increases, causing water to flow into streams more quickly and allowing less water to replenish the groundwater."

Comments:

Once again, the County refuses to acknowledge agricultural sources as a problem. When the increased runoff from "tiled" farm fields: an opaque, strong smelling liquid blend of water, sediment and agricultural contaminants; began to overflow the ditch in front of my house and spread across my lawn — the County merely dug a bigger, deeper ditch and put in a larger culvert for my driveway. Tompkins County makes no effort to reduce the runoff from agricultural fields; they just continue digging bigger ditches.

Wetland Protection

The County Comp Plan:

"At the state level, NYSDEC regulates wetlands of at least 12.4 acres in size and smaller wetlands of unusual local importance. Taken together, these regulations have the effect of leaving responsibility for regulation of isolated wetlands of less than 12.4 acres to local governments. Identification and protection of these otherwise newly unregulated wetlands is a priority."

Comments:

New York State Agricultural Law has a different priority for land use that allows *"grazing and watering livestock, making reasonable use of water resources, harvesting natural products of the wetlands, selectively cutting timber, draining land or wetlands for growing agricultural products and otherwise engaging in the use of wetlands or other land for growing agricultural products,"* thereby completely undercutting the authority of local government to protect these valuable resources.

Riparian Corridors

The County Comp Plan:

"Riparian corridors are the lands bordering streams and represent a transition zone from aquatic to terrestrial ecosystems. Maintaining lands adjacent to streams in their undeveloped state helps to support the natural functions associated with stream buffers, including protecting water quality, stabilizing stream banks and preventing erosion, trapping sediment and nutrients, improving floodwater retention and groundwater recharge, and shading stream channels in summer."

"Providing vegetated buffers of at least 100 feet either side of stream banks, or 50 feet from intermittent streams, is critical in achieving water quality benefits"

Comments:

Unfortunately, New York State NRCS agricultural manure spreading standards for CAFOs requires only 35-foot setback, where the entire setback width is a vegetated buffer; and just a 15-foot setback with incorporation within 24 hours of application to be maintained between manure applications and surface waters and surface inlets.

Well Water

The County Comp Plan:

"The amount of available drinking water is primarily an issue in rural areas that obtain drinking water from groundwater. As more homes and businesses are built in these areas, they are supported by new wells withdrawing more water from groundwater supplies. In some parts of the county it has been observed that new wells noticeably decrease the supply of water in nearby wells."

Comments:

While slamming rural families; the County's Comp Plan deliberately ignores the massive negative impact that high water-use "farming practices," especially those of CAFOs, are having on the county's groundwater supply. One CAFO owner in Minnesota reported a well water use of 570,200,000 gallons in 2017. [The average unrestricted water use for a family of four is 320 to 400 gallons a day.]

While the County's Comp Plan recommends that *"Land uses and facilities that pose the greatest threats to groundwater should be located away from areas that contribute to drinking water supplies"* — the Plan's suppression of agricultural pollution as an environmental threat reveals an unannounced policy to exclude agriculture from any County restriction or regulation.

Note: April, 2022 – a permit for a project to consolidate three mines in a rural area of the county, increase the size with an additional 46 acres, increase the depth of the mine floor to 1115', and withdraw 2,000,000 gallons of water a day; was met with no County opposition. The NYSDEC determined this action "will not have a significant effect on the environment."

Climate Change - Energy and Greenhouse Gas Emissions

The County Comp Plan:

"While global energy and climate problems cannot be solved exclusively at the local level, and leadership is needed from global, federal, and state organizations, locally we can identify, plan for, and take steps to address these issues."

"PRINCIPLE Tompkins County should be a place where the energy system meets community needs without contributing additional greenhouse gases to the atmosphere."

The Plan goes on to state:

"Emissions from residential, commercial, and industrial buildings together accounted for the largest proportion of community emissions and transportation accounted for more than a third of all community emissions."

But finally admits:

". . . it appears that it would be more accurate to use a much greater GWP for methane to reflect its

extreme potency in the shorter duration when reductions will most help in limiting warming that may result in a cascade of uncontrollable negative impacts. Such an analysis of methane will likely be incorporated into future energy plans, and would primarily affect the waste and agriculture sectors, as they are currently the highest emitters of methane."

Comments:

This admission that the "agricultural sector" is one of the "highest emitters of methane" – *is the one and only time that the Tompkins County Comprehensive Plan acknowledges the negative impact of any agricultural practice on either the residents or the environment*; and then only that this *"will likely be incorporated into future energy plans."*

The Town and City of Ithaca sit like spiders in the center of a web; with recent redistricting placing 8 of the 14 Legislative Districts at least partly within their borders.

The large student population [30% of the county's total population] gives those legislators a great deal of power; but little accountability, from a constantly shifting youthful population with no history or permanent ties to the area, and no association with the county's rural communities. This leaves county policy making vulnerable to the influence of corporate and corporately-controlled entities like Cornell University, and the Cornell Cooperative Extension.

The Tompkins County Comprehensive Plan's glaring refusal to acknowledge the reality of agricultural pollution in their reporting is clear evidence of this influence.

"Tompkins County" government is in the process of yet another legislative redistricting . . . and the Tompkins County Legislature will appoint the committee on reapportionment.

RULER OF ALL YOU SURVEY

The "telephone survey" is an excellent example of how Tompkins County authorities validate elitist policy making – while at the same time giving the appearance of meaningful public participation.

The following document uses the Town of Lansing Telephone Survey as a "How To" guide for politicians looking to legitimize "quid pro quo" government and short-circuit future opposition.

How to Create the Perfect Telephone Survey

Preparing the Survey

TIP: Telephone surveys should always be carried out early in the decision making process; before residents have a chance to consider the ramifications or discuss the issues among themselves.

It's very important to decide on the answers you want *before* formulating your questions in order to ensure a successful survey.

Include as many respondents as possible who will not be affected by the survey results.

TIP: Avoid displaying any correlation between the respondents and their answers that may weaken your case: for example – people who rent, and only moved into town for 'convenience' or plan to stay less than five years, are unlikely to care about the long-term impact of your policies and are more likely to express support.

Make sure your "random" survey has no surprises by instituting quotas of respondents for each of the different demographic categories you've created — Hang up any anybody who's been "apportioned out."

TIP: "The Devil is in the Dialogue": Don't include any questions that you don't want the answers to, and make sure to limit the choices in your "multiple-choice" questions.

Ask the most questions in the areas you want to have the greatest weight in the results. This is your primary agenda.

Add "filler": Up to 50% of the questions should be non-arguable demographic questions: this will lend an atmosphere of solidity and worth to the survey.

Generalize to avoid problem areas: the answers can be interpreted as an approval of any specific policy later.

• Don't ask — "Would you support a large increase in the school taxes?"

• Ask — "Do you want our children to receive the best quality education?" [The inclusive "our" is always a useful touch.]

Don't ask residents if they actually want something: your position is to assume it will happen and ask what they want to do with it.

• Don't ask — "Do you want a Town Center?"

• Ask — "Do you want sidewalks/a mini-mall in the Town Center?"

Ask questions in a way that is psychologically loaded:

• Don't ask — "Would you support re-zoning to allow large-scale apartment complexes?"

- Ask — "Would you support housing for families in need?"

Make sure you offer special services to the people as a "rider" so they will support your development agenda: for example – "Is the use of tax dollars for the development of recreational biking/hiking and walking trails important to you?"

Use the elderly and disabled as leverage to get what you want: for example – "Do you support use of tax dollars for [*your agenda here*] including services for the elderly and persons with disabilities."

Include the largest topic areas for your questions so that the general can override the specific: for example ask – "Agree or disagree – The roadways and intersections in the county are generally safe for pedestrians" especially if the roads in your town are not safe for pedestrians.

Presenting the Survey Results

Always stress the accuracy of the survey's methodology to mask the agenda used in the creating the questions and your interpretation of the answers.

Use "pie" and "bar" charts to lend the weight of a *scientific fact* to your presentation.

TIP: Add requests and suggestions from survey responders to make it seem as if you're interested in what the public has to say.

In Conclusion

If you have followed the preceding guidelines and recommendations, you will have all the material you need to present a clear-cut "mandate" for your project or policy. **FINAL TIP:** Make sure all the influential "partner-stakeholders" receive a cut to be certain of their continued support.

RURAL SPRAWL

"How many legs does a dog have if you call his tail a leg? Four. Saying that a tail is a leg doesn't make it a leg." — Abraham Lincoln

. . . But if you keep on insisting his tail a leg – people will start to believe you.

This is the rationale behind the creation of the term: "rural sprawl" — a term designed to obscure the truth.

Since this chapter focuses on a single example, and the area's Town and County comprehensive plans will be subject to a detailed examination in other chapters; I will merely outline the housing agenda in Tompkins County.

Ithaca; named the "Best College Town in America" is also reported as being the "8th most expensive city in the U.S. to raise a family." The ability of landlords to rent a 3 or 4-bedroom apartment to students for far more than families can afford to pay, along with the high property taxes; have pushed out the college and business workers; and artificially forced the creation of urban sprawl bedroom communities in the outlying rural towns and villages.

While Ithaca planners designate block after block of their wood frame houses as historically important and surround the city with 3,800 acres of "conservation land" — the rural town of Lansing has 0 acres of conservation land; and its secluded 33-acre Salmon Creek Bird Sanctuary has been turned into a sanctuary for drug dealers and drug users through County cut-backs.

The best way for Ithaca to preserve its gentrified way of life – while expanding the colleges and increasing their importance as a business center – was to markedly increase the size and density of their urban sprawl "satellites."

This is where the concept of "Rural Sprawl" comes in.

These sprawl bedroom communities became "identified" as *Development Focus Areas* for "compact residential development" – the County adopted a plan that categorized rural Lansing as an *Emerging Node* with the need for a municipal water and sewer infrastructure to support additional development in the area.

The awkward problem of urban sprawl – was suddenly the solution.

Increasing Tompkins County's urban resettlement was now the *only* answer to "rural sprawl": the new "Red Menace" of rural residents destroying the land, water, and future of the county.

[An interesting attribution for a rural community that had done just the opposite for over 200 years.]

The fact that "rural sprawl" and its attendant denunciations appear 11 times in the Town of Lansing Comprehensive Plan is not surprising — Cornell not only wrote the Town's Agricultural Plan; it supplied all the planning for the Town's Comp Plan as well.

By 2021; Lansing's native residents were completely disenfranchised and marginalized – with incomers taking control of the government. This is how Urban Colonialism works in Tompkins County.

The "rural sprawl" argument is a patronizing pastiche that any rigorous questioning would expose; but in a dictatorship, even a pseudo-democratic one, you can't change anything . . . and you don't ask questions.

FORM BASED CODES

What's *really* wrong with "Euclidean" zoning?

It's one area of government where people still have the right to discuss and to decide — as neighbors — and as themselves.

Form Based Code proponents want to change all that.

Form Based Codes ensure only one thing; the overriding regulatory power of authorities to enforce conformity to their wishes — once that power is given; there is no taking it back.

Like the "Nine-Point Plans" that are so beloved by agricultural polluters and their cronies — Form Based Code implementation limits the public to ineffectual commenters; with no meaningful participation or oversight in the decision making process. All the pre-planning sales talk of multi-day "charrettes" and public input is merely window dressing with no legally defined existence. Form Based Codes are designed to promote development, not to protect residents.

Contrary to common ethical standards; the discussion surrounding the adoption of Form Based Codes is limited to praising its beneficence; and never touches on its inherent flaws nor discloses the extent of its authoritarian powers.

The dream of planners: to design communities as efficient interlocking parts; and only afterward "populate" them – and the desire of authorities: to control all within their sphere [without annoying objections and obstacles] – combine in the creation of Form Based Code environments: the biggest threat to human worth and individuality since the Skinner Box.

The inclusion of *Form Based Codes* into the Town of Lansing's Comprehensive Plan strategy reveals much about the process and intent of government in Tompkins County:

The "Town of Lansing Comprehensive Plan" could more accurately be called: "Cornell's Plan for the Town of Lansing."

The complete marginalization of Lansing's residents took place in three steps:

1. Cornell's *Survey Research Institute* prepared and administered a questionable survey; the results of which were recanted during public outcry, and later quietly reinstated as the underpinning mandate for all the Town's Comprehensive Plan policy decisions.

2. Cornell's fraudulent "Rural Sprawl" domino effect scenario was adopted without debate by Lansing Town authorities; a fear provoking concoction designed to suppress rural opposition and legitimize the creation of a "mini-city" with thousands of housing units; thus artificially maintaining Ithaca's "small-town living" as an attraction for the students and professionals needed by an ever-expanding University and growing business center — and keeping thousands of acres of suitable building land in Ithaca untouched and taxes lower by placing the housing for their workers and families, and the high cost of services, in another municipality.

3. Cornell's *Design Connect* Form Based Code planning offered an unopposable regulatory power to block any possibility of resident oversight or revision.

What was the Town of Lansing's decision process for the inclusion of a Form Based Code future in their Comprehensive Plan?

A simple one:

- Cornell's *Design Connect* made a presentation that was attended by 25 residents.

- Those residents were asked for comments.

- A 27 page "sales brochure" promoting the benefits of across-the-board Form Based Code regulatory policies was added to the Comprehensive Plan without any further public involvement or approval. No alternative planning idea was given any space.

This is how things work in Tompkins County Government: authorities "identify a need" – they develop a plan – and they adopt the plan. Form Based Codes streamline the development planning and approval process by removing the public from any planning or approving — that's one more reason why politicians, planners, and developers everywhere are so enamored with this tool of power.

COMPLETE STREETS

A children's puzzle-book approach to solving real-world problems

It's NIMBY planning with Ivy League backing: Cornell's *Design Connect* Complete Streets transportation "design interventions" drop the traffic and esthetic of a "mini-city" urban sprawl bedroom community into the middle of a green rural landscape.

It's part of the University's plan to solve Ithaca's residential development and housing problems — by dumping them on someone else: the rural town of Lansing.

Cornell's *Design Connect* isn't just looking to help residents; they're advocating "changes to town policy and planning procedure" as well.

It isn't surprising that their policy recommendations echo every other "helping" voice – since it's all the same voice and the same agenda. While the *Design Connect* study uses every possible reason for increasing the construction of residential housing in Lansing; it declares that the town should: *"Limit the acreage of land zoned for commercial and light industrial uses in the Town. Dis-courage strip commercial development through appropriate zoning mechanisms. Limit heavy industry to existing Industrial/Research (IR) Districts."*

"County" planning has decided that Ithaca should be the only business center, and has actively worked to block Lansing's attempts bring businesses into town — the Tompkins County Legislature actually went to Albany to stop NYSEG from supplying Lansing with the natural gas that was needed for new commercial and industrial development.

". . . the southern portion of the town of Lansing will likely continue to serve as a bedroom community for Ithaca professionals and other workers."

Design Connect's "Best Planning Practices" not only accept the existence of a major urban sprawl bedroom community in the rural town of Lansing; they seek to greatly increase its size and density through "urban design overlay zones," and recommend that the town "increase density and provide affordable housing," change zoning with "reduced minimum open space requirements," "Density Bonuses," and "Amended Density

Requirements," – and build a new infrastructure to accommodate that increase – merely tacking on the goals of efficiency and low carbon emissions onto what is clearly *not* the "best planning practice" for a rural community.

Their recommendations for Lansing include "redevelopment of underutilized properties"; while at the same time there are block after block of old wood-frame houses in downtown Ithaca that would be perfect sites for redevelopment as high-density housing, and thousands of unused acres suitable for building surrounding the City's core.

The redevelopment of Ithaca's unused and underutilized building lots, and creation of affordable and appropriate urban housing, will solve the housing shortage, require no new infrastructures, efficiently use existing bus routes, be in the closest proximity to jobs in the education, business, institutional, and health care sectors, increase access to the cultural center of the county, and have the highest possible walkability and the greatest alternative transport choices for residents, while at the same time reducing the carbon footprint for transportation to a minimum.

It would solve every one of Lansing's housing and transportation problems but one: Cornell does not want that solution.

Everywhere; there is the exhortation for more higher-density housing in the town of Lansing: high-density housing for affordable housing, high-density housing for sustainability, high-density housing for the environment, high-density housing for lower taxes, for the aging, for reducing carbon emissions, for curing cancer, for bringing about World Peace . . . the high-density housing that is needed in rural Lansing to maintain Ithaca's gentrified, college-town pastiche for students – taking four years of memories, going to a six-figure salary, and adding more coin to Cornell's corporate coffers.

ZONE ALONE

03/18/2015 – Local Law Amended

APPENDIX II: ADULT ENTERTAINMENT
ORDINANCE

1) INTENT

"It is the intent of this local law to regulate
sexually-oriented businesses, to promote the
health, safety, morals and general welfare of the
citizens of the Town of Lansing and to establish
reasonable and uniform regulations to monitor the
location and concentration of sexually oriented
businesses within the town of Lansing."

"A sexually oriented business, as defined herein,
may be operated only within a rural agricultural
district in the TOWN OF LANSING"

Adult arcades, Adult bookstores/Adult video stores;
including Instruments, devices or paraphernalia
which are designed for use in connection with
"specified sexual activities" – Adult nightclubs and

bars, Adult theaters, Massage parlors, Escort agencies, and Sexual encounter centers.

Instead of placing this Adult Entertainment in a well-trafficked and lit commercial district; this "reasonable" law restricts all sexually-oriented businesses to an area where the families are poorer and more isolated, there is little traffic, no street lights, and no deputy's patrols — the perfect hunting ground for the kind of sexual predators these unmonitored and out of sight businesses would draw.

Why? Because, I was told by the Town Supervisor: "People in the other parts of town would get upset if it was allowed near where they lived or could be seen." No reasons for how this decision promotes "the health, safety, morals and general welfare" of rural families have ever been given.

TOWN OF LANSING COMPREHENSIVE PLAN

Part 1

Home Invasion

The rural Town of Lansing is racing ahead to be the "the growth part of the Tompkins County area," but when you look around; there's no competition in sight — so why are they doing this?

Nothing shows the duplicitous agenda of Tompkins County government as clearly as their treatment of housing. This essay will examine housing policy statements in both the Tompkins County Comprehensive Plan, and the Cornell-written Town of Lansing Comprehensive Plan.

Ithaca has been simultaneously listed as *both "the best destination for students"* in the American Institute of Economic Research's list of the best college towns in the country, and as #11 in the Top 20 cities with the *"least affordable rents"* by the New York Times.

With its high rents, high taxes, and lack of housing already forcing 80% of their workers to live outside the City, how can Ithaca attract new businesses and provide affordable housing while keeping College revenues up and protecting those low-density, high rent urban neighborhoods with that "small town feeling" students and professors love?

Answer: Force another municipality to build the affordable housing that your workers need, and let them shoulder the cost of the schools and services; while you keep the businesses and spending in your upscale, "small town" Ithaca.

Create a "vision," for Tompkins County and use all of your credentials and influence to sell it directly to another town government – and by the time the town's residents wake up to what's happening; it's too late.

The Tompkins County Comprehensive Plan's backers heavily and aggressively promote the creation of an "Urban Center" and "Development Focus Areas":

"The Urban Center includes portions of the City of Ithaca, the Towns of Ithaca and Lansing, and the Villages of Cayuga Heights and Lansing and is the largest of the Development Focus Areas."

"It is envisioned in the future at least two-thirds of all new residential development would occur in the Development Focus Areas."

The following excerpts from the comprehensive plans of the *"Urban Center"* municipalities gives a clearer picture of how this residential development will actually be shared:

Village of Lansing Comp Plan: *"All HDR [High Density Residential/Multi-Family] parcels in the Village have been developed."*

Village of Cayuga Heights Comp Plan: *"For the purpose of land use analysis, the County plan . . . anticipates no major changes for the Village in the coming decades."*

City of Ithaca Comp Plan: *"No significant changes to the character of low-density residential areas are proposed." "No significant changes to the character of medium-density residential areas are proposed"*

Town of Ithaca Comp Plan: *"The HDR–High Density Residential zone accommodates detached and semi-detached (duplex) residences in a medium density setting. . . Only 136 acres, or 0.7% of the Town, is zoned HDR."*

Town of Lansing Comp Plan:

"From these residential housing maps, we can see that the area of South Lansing, which runs along Triphammer and Warren Roads, is currently unaffordable for the majority of people within the region. However, due to close proximity to jobs, shopping and the university it would make for an ideal location for housing, which would provide the opportunity for people to earn a living and spend less than the 30% threshold for affordability."

Since the rural Town of Lansing is the farthest municipality in the County's new "urban center" – 8 miles – from Cornell and Ithaca's business and shopping: arguing this development on the basis of its "close proximity" and "ideal location" is more than a misrepresentation.

"By creating compact neighborhoods of high population density, TCAT would be more likely to expand into this area and thereby making housing more affordable by eliminating the costs of additional vehicles and associated transportation."

How can you argue to expand mass transit into a new area; when you already have an existing transit system *and* great walkability in an urban area with endless housing redevelopment potential? An area that has the jobs and businesses that these relocated workers would need to be bused many extra miles to get to.

"Housing expansion in the form of new developments and PUD's will result in increased traffic and the need to expand roads and/or mass transit to accommodate the resulting increase in population. As with municipal water and sewer, the logical choice would be to gradually expand out from the village into the area of South Lansing and eventually further north."

[PUDs are "Planned Unit Developments" - a term used to describe a housing development that is not subject to standard zoning requirements for the area – a further erosion of any community control.]

Since the Town of Lansing will need to "create neighborhoods," "expand roads," and add "municipal water and sewer" to their infrastructure, as well as being miles further away from Ithaca's job and business center than any other municipality in the County's "Urban Center" plan — how could this ever be considered the best planning solution for Tompkins County?

Town of Lansing 2018 Comprehensive Plan's "Proposed Future Land Uses": depicts thousands of acres that will be zoned for apartments and condominiums. Tompkins County and "Lansing's" government plan to turn a once rural town into the largest and most concentrated collection of housing developments in the region.

"The construction of a new four-lane highway on the outskirts of Ithaca, NY created a rapidly growing commercial center in the previously rural Town of Lansing. The clash between the newcomers and the old-timers over the direction and pace of this change led to the formation of a new local government and the incorporation of the Village of Lansing." – Lansing at the Crossroads: A Partisan History of the Village of Lansing*, New York, Rita Smidt*

Incomers from Ithaca and Cornell continued to move into what was left of rural Lansing; creating a large urban sprawl bedroom community and gradually taking over the town's government and planning. Finding a loophole from an old agreement to share municipal Highway Dept. services: that allowed residents of the Village of Lansing to vote in the Town of Lansing's elections without any reciprocity – they blanketed the Village's streets with election signs calling themselves the candidates "For All of Lansing" — there were no ethical qualms about having residents from a different municipality, with a very different viewpoint, voting into office a Town Board that would radically change the community they had historically "clashed" with. The plan worked.

It's the Fall of 2021; and upcoming elections for Lansing's Town Board – a sign in the Village of Lansing:

PLEASE VOTE!

Village of Lansing

residents

vote in

Lansing Town Elections

First Tuesday in November

After all; isn't this in line with the ethics and actions already demonstrated by Tompkins County government itself?

The *"Urban Center/Development Focus Area/Rural Sprawl"* housing agenda that County Planners concocted for the Town of Lansing is an example of everything that's wrong with the *"City-centric"* planning of Tompkins County today:

• Academic credentials at the service of vested interests.

• Adopting a lesser plan to appease a greater master.

And maybe what's even worse; in a college "destination" with such smug pretensions of being a seat of learning and illumination — it's intellectually dishonest.

THE MAP IS NOT THE TERRITORY

The mapmakers are

Sometimes it can be little things that point the most clearly to misconduct and undue influence in government policy making.

Removed from the shadows of bureaucratic justification: each piece tells a story of the ethics and intent behind these public policies — who receives the benefits — and how that affects the life of the community.

In this chapter; I will use the legal definition of fraud to examine a map that was used to support far-reaching policy decisions, summarize the results of that examination and its disclosure

The map is the "Town of Lansing, N.Y. Agricultural Property" map displaying the legend: "Agricultural Exemptions 2016". The source is "Tompkins County Assessment Dept, 2016" and it contains the seal and imprint of the "Tompkins County Planning Dept".

Fraud is commonly understood as *dishonesty calculated for advantage*. It can be proved by showing that the defendant's actions involved five separate elements:

(1) A false statement of a material fact

Nearly half of the land marked as "agricultural property" in this map is not owned by agricultural entities; and is only rented for agricultural use. Much of this property is residential or commercially owned and rented for a little tax relief – in a county that has one of the highest median property taxes in the United States.

Although the map purports to show "Agricultural Exemptions" - much of the land marked does not receive any agricultural exemption. For example: only 40% of my neighbor's land received an agricultural exemption; but 100% was marked as receiving it in this map.

(2) Knowledge on the part of the defendant that the statement is untrue

In a "clarification" email; the County's Assessment Department admitted that they knowingly helped create a map misrepresenting the actual acreage receiving Agricultural Exemptions: "The intention of the map is to show the parcels that receive an agricultural exemption – it is not intended to show how much of each parcel receives an exemption." Although this is clearly not the representation of this map; the Assessment Dept. still insisted: "The map is in fact correct."

(3) Intent on the part of the defendant to deceive the alleged victim

This map was used to support preferential agricultural policies for a handful of influential farmers, including the unilateral creation of an Agricultural Zone, to the exclusion and detriment of 95% of the existing rural community — an intentional misrepresentation of material existing fact. This is an "afterthought" piece of supporting evidence; created and added after the town's Agriculture Protection Plan was already approved – what it claims to be is clearly, knowingly, and admittedly, not a true representation.

(4) Justifiable reliance by the alleged victim on the statement

This map is "signed off" on by both the County Assessment Dept. and the County Planning Dept.; it was included in the Town's comprehensive plan, and was presented with those credentials as a factual representation. Residents were invited to place reliance on this map and approve the rezoning of half of the town from Rural/Agricultural to Agricultural only.

(5) Injury to the alleged victim as a result

This map was used by authorities to justify the enactment of restrictive policies against "non-farming" residents; further marginalizing the county's rural poor — to promote Agriculture as the only preferred use of rural land, and to designate farmers as the sole and exclusive "stakeholders" in the rural community.

This map is included in the arguments of Town and County "representatives" who fostered citizen petitions to prevent the sale or rental of rural land for solar farms or for housing, and force highly-taxed rural landowners to sell cheaply to farmers; already the richest and most influential people in the community. The "consolidation" of rural land into the hands of ever-larger farming corporations; further enables the spread of "modern farming methods" that have been proven to cause "significant harm" to neighboring families.

A knowingly inaccurate map should neither have been created nor have been offered for inclusion in the Town's Comprehensive Plan – a legal document that is described in NY Town Law as: "Among the most important powers and duties granted by the legislature to a town government."

Additionally, whereas this map is offered as a proof of intent by the Town to protect land for continued agricultural use; the Town has sold the land that it rented for agriculture use to a housing developer — and a different Comprehensive Plan map shows that the Town plans to zone most of the agricultural land in the southern half of town for future residential and commercial development.

Just changing the legend and/or name of the map would only cover up the situation and retain any advantages that the misrepresentation has already given to the parties involved.

I sent these arguments in an email requesting that the County Legislature remove this map from its files and from any documents wherein it has been used, and to correct as much as possible the damage its use has caused.

Attachments included both the Agricultural Property map and the "clarification" email from the County Assessment Department.

There was no response or acknowledgement from any of the county's 14 Legislators.

If it is ethics that give a government legitimacy; what does the County's creation and continued use of this map represent?

The Town of Lansing's 2016 Agricultural Property map is just one example of the deliberate misrepresentations that riddle the County's planning agenda.

TOWN OF LANSING COMPREHENSIVE PLAN

From First to Last

Buried towards the end of Chapter 4 in the *Town of Lansing Comprehensive Plan*; is a paragraph that should have come at the plan's beginning – a statement that reveals the true authorship and intent of the town's future policy making:

"The best way to plan for the long-term future of the Town of Lansing is to decide regionally where the major commercial, educational, shopping, recreational, health care, agricultural, manufacturing and residential sectors will be located. The reality is that our municipalities are not in competition with each other; rather they survive in symbiotic relationships. We should build upon these cooperative relationships in land-use decisions as well, while respecting a town's right to home rule. New York State Law delegates planning decisions to the town and city levels but does not forbid a more coordinated process."

This statement unilaterally rewrites the whole structure of responsibility and obligation of town government; and directly contradicts New York State Town Law § 272-a:

"The development and enactment by the town government of a town comprehensive plan which can be readily identified, and is available for use by the public, is in the best interest of the people of each town."

The Law clearly shows the intent of the law is NOT to make the Town's comprehensive plan a *"regional"* decision.

"Among the most important powers and duties granted by the legislature to a town government is the authority and responsibility to undertake town comprehensive planning"

The comprehensive plan is an *important "duty"* and *"responsibility"* of the town government – and as such cannot be delegated or subordinated to other agencies or interests.

"The participation of citizens in an open, responsible and flexible planning process is essential to the designing of the optimum town comprehensive plan."

The Town of Lansing planning process was anything but *"open";* with citizen participation relegated to a scattering of meaningless pre-planning activities – *and offering NO participation for residents throughout the entire decision-making and policy approval process.*

Lansing Town Government's claims of public representation rests on a single telephone survey, prepared and administered by *Cornell University's Survey Research Institute (SRI)* [See *Ruler of All you Survey* for a more detailed examination.] – A survey that was widely attacked by Lansing residents in a Town Meeting. The advocates of the survey retreated – and ended up by claiming that it was only meant to give an indication, and was not to be considered an important policy document. This same survey was later cited and used throughout the final Comprehensive Plan as both a definitive source and as a mandate from the town's residents.

In this "Community Survey" – 365 town residents were cold-called on issues that had never been brought up for discussion or debate, to reply to a series questions that showed a definite bias in their preparation.

137

The Survey's method of formulation and its inclusion as the Town's only source of policy-defining public participation – shows the ongoing misrepresentation of policy goals and lack of ethical underpinning that pervades policy-making in Tompkins County.

New York State Town Law § 272-a:

*"In the event the town board prepares a proposed town comprehensive plan or amendment thereto, the town board shall hold one or more public hearings and such other meetings as it deems necessary **to assure full opportunity for citizen participation in the preparation of such proposed plan or amendment"***

Everybody I talk to; everybody; believes that there is no meaningful participation by the people in either Town or County government — and the actions of government policy-makers to stubbornly continue insisting that there *is* meaningful public participation; while refusing to allow public participation and oversight; gives legitimacy to that belief.

The lead writer of the Town of Lansing Agriculture and Farmland Protection Plan [from *Cornell Cooperative Extension*] publicly expressed the opinion that nobody but farmers "deserved to live in north Lansing" [an opinion that no Town official would rebut] – And the entire Plan was prepared while excluding 95% of the rural residents from any participation at all. This "Protection Plan" [including its policy of rural citizen exclusion] was then approved by both the Town of Lansing, and Tompkins County governments – and became an important part of the Town's Comprehensive Plan's "vision."

It's should be interesting for students of Tompkins County government to note how perfectly both the Ag Protection Plan and the Lansing Comp Plan dovetail together — with both supporting each other and claiming that the other Plan is essential to the success of their own.

Unsurprisingly; the 2018 Town of Lansing Comprehensive Plan echoes the exact same policies and concerns as the Tompkins County Comprehensive Plan of three years earlier: Lansing Town Government has abjured their duty to the people of the town — and meekly acquiesced to the County's primacy by accepting "planning at the county level".

The Town of Lansing should post a disclaimer on all their documents stating: *"No meaningful public participation was used in the formulation of these policies and regulations."*

AG PROTECTION PLAN

Title VI – Take the High Road

Impenetrable is the word that best describes Tompkins County government's policy making. From their "identifying needs," and continuing through their entire policy formulation and approval process — there is no place where the public has any meaningful participation; or *any* participation. County and local government decision making is as far out of reach of the rural residents as a royal coach parading past the commoners.

The *Town of Lansing Agriculture and Farmland Protection Plan* is a good example of how well government is defended from public intrusion; even at the local level — and how each level is supported and protected by every succeeding level of authority.

In response to my email expressing concerns with the "Summary of Findings" section of the Proposed Agriculture and Farmland Protection Plan, after my opening comment:

"This Summary gives overall feeling that nobody else lives [or deserves to live] in North Lansing but farmers."

M** R** [Cornell Cooperative Extension's Agricultural Issue Leader — and the Plan's lead writer] inserted the phrase:

"- you are right"

This blatant statement of planning bias was never retracted or contradicted by CCE, or any subsequent authority, at any level of government.

Title VI Complaint

12/21/2015 – I completed a Formal Complaint/CCE Tompkins County form and mailed it via Certified Mail to K** S** [Association Executive Director and CCE Title VI Coordinator.]

Opening summary of the Complaint's issues:

Re: Complaint Under Title VI Environmental Justice

I submit this complaint against Cornell Cooperative Extension Tompkins County for issuing a report [The

Town of Lansing Agriculture and Farmland Protection Plan] and associated documents under the heading "Ag Documents" recommending the creation of an Agricultural Zone with significant zoning changes that will have a disproportionately negative impact on the poor non-farming residents of that district.

The Environmental Justice Community identification methodology was flawed. CCE Tompkins never [EJ] mapped the actual Ag Zone. The boundaries and inclusion/exclusion of land in the Lansing Agricultural Zone is arbitrary and capricious. The mandates for meaningful participation were consistently ignored. The non-farming residents [95% of the district's population] were entirely and deliberately excluded from the report writing and making process. Plan information released was deceptive and false. The CCE Tompkins County Agricultural Issue Leader was clearly and admittedly biased. No venue or public meeting for rebuttal of the Plan's assertions and policies was ever held. No disclosure of the negative impact of the Plan's policies and recommendations on non-farming residents was ever made. No outreach was made to advertise or inform the non-farming

143

residents of the Plan's public hearing. Plan's assertions were never questioned, or allowed to be questioned. No questions of any kind were allowed at the public hearing. The committee appointed for "setting the plan into motion and prioritizing the actions" will be composed entirely of farmers and agricultural landowners, preventing non-farming residents from having any say in the future of their own community.

"The Environmental Justice component of Title VI guarantees fair treatment for all people and provides for Cornell Cooperative Extension of Tompkins County (CCE — Tompkins), to identify and address, as appropriate, disproportionately high and adverse effects of its programs, policies, and activities on minority and low-income populations"

The body of the Complaint identified and detailed numerous defects in the Plan; where it knowingly and deliberately ignored mandates for meaningful participation:

The EPA's goal for Environmental Justice:

"the fair treatment and meaningful involvement of all people" with *"particular emphasis on the public*

health of and environmental conditions affecting minority, low-income, and indigenous populations"

The DEC:

The creation of a zoning district is a "permitting" activity. [NYSDEC CP-29] "This policy will promote the fair involvement of all people in the DEC environmental permit process."

The Complaint also listed Ag Plan Committee actions that would further disenfranchise the rural poor by removing their ability to participate the future of their own community.

The Conclusion of the Complaint:

"In spite of their claims of 'Building Strong and Vibrant New York Communities,' their Title VI mandates and the publicly stated policies of New York State; Cornell Cooperative Tompkins County deliberately excluded the very community they've chosen to bear all of these health, monetary and life costs from the decision making process of this Plan.

Public participation is intended to provide legitimacy to government decisions — excluding 95% of the people speaks for itself."

I would like to be able to write about how these issues were argued and adjudicated; but I can't — because I never found out.

This is how it all went down:

The Formal Complaint was received and signed for at CCE Tompkins on 12/21/2015 – but I was unable to get a response to my emails until 1/21/2016 and finally arranged a meeting on **2/8/2016** with the CCE Title VI Coordinator.

He said he would read through the Ag Plan; and spoke of a revised Plan with the representation of all rural residents.

2/9/2016 – my follow up email was unacknowledged.

2/22/2016 – 2/29/2016 – 3/9/2016 – follow up emails were all unacknowledged.

3/28/2016 – Title VI Complaint with cover letter was mailed via Certified Mail to CCE Director C** W**.

Reply dated 5/3/2016 – from CCE Director C** W**:

*"In reviewing the information you shared with S*** *and information contained within the Agriculture*

and Farmland Protection Plan we have come to the conclusion that the responsible party for the plan is the Town of Lansing. We ask that you direct your complaint to the Town of Lansing as this is their plan and responsibility."

6/21/2016 – Letters with enclosures were mailed via Certified Mail to Town of Lansing Supervisor and Town Board members [and copied with enclosures to three Senators.]

Replies from two Senators: "I do not have authority or jurisdiction to intervene . . . the Town of Lansing would have the final decision in this matter." "Your situation involves city agencies and is, therefore, under the jurisdiction of your local government officials."

There was never any acknowledgement or reply to this letter from any of my "local government officials."

8/4/2016 – Follow up letters were mailed via Certified Mail to Town of Lansing Supervisor and Town Board members regarding their lack of response to requests for meaningful participation by rural residents.

There was never any acknowledgement or reply to this letter.

Like a narrow pathway winding around the outside of a towering stone barricade – taking the "high road" to public participation brought me ever-higher – but never closer to my goal.

The "high road" leads nowhere.

CHIPPING AWAY AT BUREAUCRACY

(Condensed from the series in *Cornithaca County*)

Most people would probably agree that government help would be better with more of the "help" and less of the "government." Our government is quick to proclaim the good of everything it does; and just as quick to find fault with anything that threatens its power.

Wouldn't it be great to have a job that only requires you to work on problems, not to solve them? This the job description our government has written for itself.

Lines of Defense

If you have ever tried to question policy decisions, stop legislation, or just find out what's going on in your local government; you've probably come up against a formidable array of bureaucratic barriers.

The following is a list of the most common defenses, and the order in which they are usually applied:

149

1. Discredit the Person

2. Discredit the Facts

3. Discredit the Situation

4. It's Legal Anyway

"Lines of Defense" will discuss these techniques and give examples of how they are used to sap the energy of any opposition.

The essay will also cover four authoritarian attitudes you will encounter: "The Silence," "The Refusal," "The Referral," and "The Questioning."

It's a battle where every time you type in a letter, they can hit the "backspace" button.

In our government's protective reflex to swat away any annoyance, its first response is to "Discredit the Person" who is causing the trouble.

This is an action that I'm quite familiar with. [See *Deadly Drift*] After being sprayed with Roundup by an agricultural boom sprayer while mowing my lawn on a windy day [and vomiting up my stomach all over the bathroom floor that night]; I made a compliant to the NYSDEC with the following result:

Their report, that required a FOIL request to access, claimed I was "politically active against farming" even though I had rented the field being sprayed to a farmer for more than 25 years, and found my actions suspicious – leaving it open that I was lying or somehow at fault myself. None of the factual data, such as the wind speed on the day of a herbicide drift complaint, was ever addressed. The report ended with "case closed!"

When it comes to discrediting the facts that conflict with and undermine government policy making decisions; authorities can choose from a number of passive and proactive methods. A bureaucratic favorite is to present the public with background information that deliberately misrepresents, and even omits key facts; in order to validate their chosen course of action.

In their *Harmful Algal Blooms (HABs): Preventing HABs* public document; the NYSDEC never once mentions agriculture as a source of nutrient pollution, although it contributes *more than four times the nutrient pollution of every other source combined* to the waters of the Finger Lakes – employing terms like "exactly predict" and "fully understand" to justify this deliberate omission.

They *do* mention that "the amount of nutrients can be decreased by: Limiting lawn fertilization" and "Maintaining septic tanks" – that contribute less than 1% to the nutrient pollution total.

If getting government authorities to admit the facts is difficult; getting them to accurately report a situation and make appropriate policy decisions is almost impossible. Not only do they occupy a "high ground" that allows them to cite everything from jobs to jurisprudence as an excuse; they can change the ground rules to suit their objectives.

A good example can be found in New York's Finger Lakes, where the region's most powerful interests are allowed to do almost all of the polluting. Since cleaning up the lakes would restrict the operations and profits of these interests; authorities have decided on a policy that merely maintains the pollution at a profitable level – a level that retains just some of the uses of these lakes. A Total Daily Maximum Load [TMDL] of pollution will be decided, and then divided among these interests, who will "try" to meet the target goals. [Cornell: one of the larger polluters, and heavily tied to agricultural interests, will establish the TDML – so all the "pollution-reduction" planning can be kept comfortably "in-house."]

This policy will cause many rural people to lose the lakes as a source of drinking water, but all the important residents [and decision makers] are on municipal water anyway; and taxes will be levied to make sure they get the proper treatment.

An important part of today's regulatory process is how well it works to protect the interests of those who are regulated. Our government continually legislates ineffectual environmental regulations; that effectively protect the polluters.

The media never questions or exposes the laws that have been created to allow polluters to knowingly and repeatedly cause harm to people and the environment. The following court decision concerns an incident took place only a few miles from my house:

The United States Court of Appeals for the Second Circuit [Mather v. Willet Dairy] in finding against plaintiffs suffering from the effects of manure off-gassing that included brain damage in one child and required surgical removal of eyelids in an adult commented that the laws *"may be inadequate for ensuring the safety of our environment and for protecting citizens from serious injury. But that is the remedy that Congress has provided and to which we are bound."*

Willet Dairy was shielded by its "permit shield" from any citizen suits – the rural victims were shielded by nothing.

The Questioning: This is the point in the denial process where the experienced bureaucrat launches a barrage of questions; trying to find fault with anything in your argument, while looking for a handle they can use. If you find yourself the focus of authoritarian questions, ask some yourself: like "If this is an accurate description of the situation and

154

these facts are confirmed; what can you do to help us correct it?" This may give you a little breathing room. [Be sure to have your own questions ready.]

The Refusal: When power is concentrated like it is in Tompkins County, it stands untouchable. No matter how much evidence is gathered, no matter how much misconduct is involved, the County's elite can slam the door shut on any activist: They refuse to investigate, they refuse to enforce the law, they refuse acknowledge, they refuse to start, they refuse to stop; they just refuse — and what can you do about that?

"The Silence" and *"The Referral"* are classic bureaucratic tools for frustrating any troublemaker who upsets the smooth flow of government routine. You may be taking time out of your life, but this is their life, and they're being paid for every minute they delay, equivocate, or redirect. It's not surprising that you may keep leaving unanswered voicemails, texts, and emails and they are "out of the office until. . ." or "in a meeting" so regularly when you show up in person or try to work your way up the departmental ladder — a bureaucrat who does

nothing is doing nothing wrong. And when you have finally caught up with the fugitive functionary; all the sweat of your effort may be turned to ice by "The Referral."

It takes only a few seconds and a few words to send you off to fill out additional forms, lobby higher-ups for their approval, or to track down someone in some other department who is even more inaccessible and difficult to get in touch with. I have had the experience of being passed around in an inescapable circle of referrals; back to the same office and the same person I started with weeks before.

"The Referral" can be the most difficult of all obstacles to overcome.

Postscript

Today's Progressives are everything that Liberals once claimed to hate and despise. Progressive policies and doctrine directly contradict the lives and beliefs of Lincoln, of Martin Luther King, Jr., of Frederick Douglass, of Mother Teresa, of Malcolm X: policies and doctrine that place human worth and equality in the hands of an all-powerful Centrality — to dispense whenever and however it wishes.

Tompkins County is overwhelmingly Progressive in doctrine; and unassailable in political power — and yet those with the education, wealth and influence; have chosen to bully, abuse, and drive out a marginalized and poor rural population: taking their land, destroying their communities – unashamedly proclaiming a vision in which those people do not, and cannot exist.

Lincoln said: "Nearly all men can stand adversity, but if you want to test a man's character, give him power."

In Tompkins County: the stones of dictatorship are too well fitted to let in any light.